Gloves
Valerie Cumming

The Costume Accessories Series
General Editor: Dr Aileen Ribeiro

Distributed by

DRAMA BOOK PUBLISHERS

821 Broadway   New York, New York   10003

ISBN 0 7134 1008 6

Typeset by Tek-Art Ltd, London SE25
and printed in Great Britain by
The Anchor Press Ltd
Tiptree, Essex
for the publishers
B.T. Batsford Ltd
4 Fitzhardinge Street
London W1H 0AH

Contents

Acknowledgment

My interest in gloves was aroused when I was given the opportunity of working with the Spence Collection of the Worshipful Company of Glovers at the Museum of London between 1975 and 1978. I am immeasurably grateful to my colleagues at the museum, and to members of the Glovers Company for encouraging my interest and assisting me in my work on the collection.

I would like to extend my thanks to the many people who have helped with my research over the last six years, in particular Miss Christine Bloxham of Oxfordshire County Museum, Miss Penelope Byrde of the Museum of Costume, Bath, Mr G.J. Carter and Mr R. Jeffries of Dent Fownes Ltd, Miss Fiona Clark of Worthing Museum, Miss Elizabeth Ann Coleman of Brooklyn Museum, New York, Mr Jeremy Farrell of the Museum of Costume and Textiles, Nottingham, Mrs Karen Finch of the Textile Conservation Centre, Hampton Court, Miss Louise Hamer of the Laing Art Gallery, Newcastle, Miss Santina Levey of the Victoria and Albert Museum, Miss Sarah Levitt, Dr Aileen Ribeiro of the Courtauld Institute of Art, Mr Derek Riley of Focal Point Ltd, Mrs Elizabeth Sandford Gunn of the Ashmolean Museum, Oxford, and Miss Kay Staniland and Mrs Vanda Foster of the Museum of London.

I am grateful to Olivia Bland who produced a clear typescript from a disordered manuscript and who also spotted various grammatical errors. Finally I would like to thank Timothy Auger, Mimi Rolbant and Clare Sunderland of Batsford for all their practical help on the editing and picture research for this book, and my husband for accepting good humouredly the domestic chaos that grew around us while it was being written.

List of Illustrations

Introduction

'Why gloves?' a friend asked me when I said I was writing this book. A perfectly valid question, which is difficult to answer concisely. Today gloves, if worn at all, are primarily a functional accessory. When I visited a distinguished glove manufacturer in the West Country it was a cold, crisp and sunny day. 'Ideal glove weather' he said approvingly, and in the subsequent discussion it became clear that in a world where gloves are no longer an indispensable accessory, the weather is an important consideration. Warm, wet winters are not good for the glove trade, and in the summer gloves are rarely worn at all, so dry, bitterly cold winters are welcomed, as being 'good for the trade'.

This is a sad reversal. For several hundred years gloves were worn throughout the year, they were bought in dozens rather than in pairs, and they came in a wide range of materials, colours, styles and sizes. Some of these gloves of the past have found their way into public or private collections, as illustrations of the past glories of the glove trade. They are comparatively easy to collect, store and display, but they are not as easy to date accurately.

It was partly the lack of reference material which prompted this book, but it was also inspired by the belief that once a wider audience has the opportunity to see some of the beautiful gloves which were once taken for granted, it might persuade them to take more care and interest in contemporary gloves. The complicated processes involved in the production of fine gloves deserve more appreciation than is presently allotted to them.

Previous glove historians have concentrated their energies on producing books or articles on specific periods, or the associations which gloves have had in regard to legal contracts, service, duty and the ceremonial life of the Church or the State. Such information is of interest to the social historian, but it is tantalizingly oblique for the costume historian. There is no straightforward, reliable guide to the successive styles of gloves which appeared from the early seventeenth century onwards, and this short book is intended to fill the vacuum.

Within the confines of a short book it is necessary to stress certain elements at the expense of others. Given the useful, if not considerable, literature on the historical significance of gloves, it seemed wise to place major emphasis on the changing glove fashions within a context of the contemporary attitudes towards their production, purchase, and the social etiquette which influenced their wearers. In addition, as a preface to this discussion, a chapter considering the actual processes which are involved in glovemaking is included as necessary information for the reader who wishes to appreciate the gloves of the past.

The period which this book covers, 1600-1980, is a wide span of time. However, like many other components of fashionable dress, gloves have passed through periods when they were particularly important accessories, but they also went through fallow periods when they required less definition and description. These pendulum swings are reflected in this book, as is the change which gradually came over all fashionable items. Men's clothes and accessories in particular became simpler and understated, leaving the frivolous and amusing fashions to women.

So, why gloves? Because they, at their finest, provided a witty, amusing and elegant counterpoint to the general fashions of a period, and because today they are so understated that many people have no conception of their long and richly varied history.

1

How Gloves Were Made

Curiosity about the fashions of the past is a constant element in contemporary society. People are intrigued, impressed or repelled by the garments worn by their ancestors, and, given the opportunity, they will attempt to satisfy their curiosity by pursuing information about what they have seen. Questions they might want answered will include such details as the cost of individual garments, the cleaning methods of the past, and the discomfort of such fashions. It is rarer to find curiosity about the production of the garments. Possibly the answers seem a matter of common sense when the major skills appear to be those of cutting and sewing; or possibly it is thought that the production process will be uninteresting, or will require an understanding of technical details which are superfluous to an appreciation of the finished article. Neither of these assumptions is true, and any attempt to trace the history of gloves over a period of nearly four hundred years without discussing this aspect would be to deny the reader a fascinating story, full of intrigue, competition and technical change, as glovemaking evolved gradually from a craft into an industry.

At the beginning of the seventeenth century it was possible to buy all three types of glove that are available to us today, namely leather, fabric and knitted gloves, although at this date their production and distribution were handled by different crafts and trades. All three types, and their simpler cousin, the mitten, were made from the skins, yarns and cloth which were known at the time. In examining the history of each variety, it will be seen that the major changes occurred when a new technical process or a different type of dressed leather, yarn or cloth became generally available to the glovemakers.

THE PRODUCTION OF LEATHER GLOVES
It is important to understand something of the complicated processes which take an animal skin from its natural state through to the pairs of gloves which are sold in the shops. Two earlier twentieth-century writers on gloves quoted 72 and 86 different processes

as being required in this transformation.[1] Both are probably correct, as it is unlikely that they visited the same factories or watched identical types of leather being processed, cut and stitched. Despite the brevity of the following explanation, it is hoped that the reader will understand enough of these complex processes to be able to appreciate the skill and length of time which elapses between the moment an animal is skinned and the time when the gloves are ready for distribution.

The traditional skins used in gloving are taken from deer, kids, goats, lambs and sheep. Other types of skin have been used in various parts of the world, and, at different periods, have been particularly fashionable. These will be mentioned in later chapters. In Great Britain the native skins used for glovemaking at the beginning of the seventeenth century were taken from deer, lambs and sheep. Kidskins, already dressed and ready for the glovemaker's shears, were imported from France.

Leather dressing, the process which turns skins into workable leather, was a traditional by-product of livestock rearing throughout the country, and the earliest glovemakers were leather dressers, although glovers had established their claim to a separate craft by the reign of Edward IV. Only certain types of skin were suitable for gloves. Dealers in animal hides (fellmongers) would sell to a variety of craftsmen who worked in leather. The fellmongers of Bampton in Oxfordshire sold skins, in the 1670s, which were 'made into jackets, breeches, leather linings and gloves'.[2] It was the specialized process of skin dressing and the skill of the dressers which provided high-quality leather more suited to glovemaking than jackets or breeches.

The fashionable members of English society always admired French kid gloves because the quality of the leather, and the elasticity of the glove, which was important in ensuring a good fit before glove calibres were invented in the nineteenth century, were far superior to the English varieties. However, even this problem could be overcome by a skilful skin dresser who was prepared to experiment with the methods he used to finish the leather. In his diary entry for 8 September 1667 Pepys noted, '. . . I met Sir G. Downing, who would speak with me; and, first to enquire what I paid for my Kids leather gloves I had on my hands, and showed me others on his, as handsome, as good in all points, cost him but 12d a pair, and mine me 2s. He told me he had been seven years

finding out a man that could dress English sheepskin as it should be; and endeed, it is now as good in all respects as Kidd, and he says will save 100,000 l. a year that goes out to France for Kidd skins. Thus he labours very worthily to advance our own trade, but doth it with mighty vanity and talking.'[3] Either Sir G. Downing's skin dresser never passed on his secret, or Pepys' French kid gloves were not of the finest quality, because French kid continued to be the fashionable leather for town gloves, despite the high duty on imported skins, and the ban, often evaded by smugglers, on the importation of French gloves (fig. 1).

Skins are either dressed on the hair or grain side, or on the flesh side. French kid skins were dressed on the grain side because the animals had skins which, when dressed, were so free of defects and so tightly grained that a smooth finish was assured. Deer, sheep and lambskins were coarser and consequently they were usually finished on the flesh side. This produced a suede finish, and lacked the superior smoothness of kid. In the nineteenth and twentieth centuries other finishes were introduced, but at this stage it is only necessary to grasp the difference between so-called dressed skins (hair or grain side) and undressed skins (flesh side).

Skin dressing yards need a plentiful supply of soft water, so they were always positioned near a clear river or a natural spring or stream. The skins arrived at the yard in a dirty, greasy condition and before they could be dressed they had to be thoroughly cleaned and then the skin had to be re-conditioned. Briefly, the processes were as follows. The skins were soaked in water for some time to remove a good deal of the oil and dirt. Then the hair was removed with a lime paste applied to the flesh side of the skin, then, after a further washing, the skins were placed in slaked lime pits for several weeks to loosen any residual hairs, skin cells and odd particles of flesh. These loosened scraps were scraped off with a knife once the lime had been washed away.

At this stage it was possible to spot any defects in the skin, and to gauge its possible use. Further washing removed the last traces of lime before the skins were rendered soft and supple by being soaked in a solution of warm water, to which the mildly ammonia additive of manure was added. After another bath of clean water, they were placed in a fermentation tub containing warm water with wheaten flour or bran.

ant tous *Jcy quelque Lingere à faute de fuccez*

◁ 1 *'Galerie of the Palace', by A. Bosse, c. 1637. Fashionable French men and women bought small luxury items from specialist makers, including plain and decorated gloves; a similar range would have been available in England.*

At this stage the skins became swollen and rose to the surface in a pulpy and pliable state. A final rinse and scraping off of any last traces of scum, short hairs and lime left the skins 'in the white'.

In the late nineteenth and twentieth centuries many of these processes became mechanized, and natural additives like lime and manure were replaced by chemicals, so that today the whole process is much quicker and requires far fewer workers. This is also true of the secondary process of skin dressing, the tawing or tanning process.

However, the three traditional methods of dressing the skins were with oil, alum or vegetable extracts such as bark or berries. Sometimes combinations of two processes were used. Oil tanning, originally called 'chamoising' because it had been employed to produce soft leather from chamois skins, required the grain surface to be scraped away to allow oil to enter from both sides. The wet skins were saturated with cod liver oil or some other fish oil and then energetically pummelled until the oil was absorbed. This process was repeated several times, then the skins were piled in a warm place to allow the oil to oxidize and combine with the animal fibres. The skins were then washed and dried, and the leather produced from this process was, in certain circumstances, washable.

The mixture of alum, salt, egg yolks, flour and perhaps a vegetable oil or fat preserved and lubricated the skins, and was mixed with water to produce a solution in which the skins were soaked for a number of days. When the skins were removed and allowed to dry, usually in a warm place, they were so dry and stiff that they needed staking. This involved passing the flesh side of the skin backwards and forwards over a staking knife until it became a supple, workable material. When skins were bark tanned they were steeped in extracts made from oak or chestnut or other tree barks, and this type of solution both dressed and dyed the skins, so that after staking they were ready, after a period of storage to allow the tannage to mature, for the glover.

Alum tanned gloves were either left 'white' or brush dyed. Great skill was required to produce an even finish, and additional lubrication, in the form of egg yolks (which do not stain skins), had to be applied after dyeing, and yet more staking was then required. The skins were then pared to an even thickness.

When the glover bought skins, he knew that the average size skin from a particular animal would yield a certain number of pairs of gloves. For instance, an imported kidskin might yield up to one and a half pairs, a lambskin would vary between one and two pairs, but a sheepskin could provide up to three or more pairs.

Cutting gloves was the most skilled of all the processes involved in the actual production of gloves. Skins were assessed for their spread, or flexibility, and then cut so that the wastage was minimal. In *The London Tradesman*, published in 1747, advice is given on the various trades in which parents might buy apprenticeships for their sons. One chapter describes the glover, who ' . . . deals in a Species of Leather different from the Shoe-Maker: The Skins he uses are not tanned, but allumm'd; for which Reason that Kind is generally called Allum Leather. He makes Gloves of Sheep, Kid and Doe Skins, and makes Breeches of Shamy (a Species of Sheep Skin differently dressed from the other) and of Buck Skin. The Glover and Breeches-Maker are sometimes separate Trades: but they are oftener together. The Glover lines Gloves with Furs and Rabbit Skins, and sometimes sells Muffs and Tippets of Fur and Ermine. Both Glover and Breeches-Maker are a Species of the Taylor; their chief Instruments being the Sheers and Needle. As to the Glover, the Hands employed in London in making them are but few, and a good many of them Women; The Glover cuts them out into their several Sizes and gives them out to be sewed at so much a Pair: A Good Hand may get Ten or Twelve Shillings a Week. The Shops are most supplied from the Country, the best from Scotland: The Irish excell in Kid-Skin; but the Duty makes them come dear. This Art requires neither much strength nor Ingenuity; only as it is a sedentary stooping Business it disagrees with a consumptive or Pthysicky Disposition.'[4]

Although this description tells us little about the actual process of glovemaking, and contains the types of inaccuracies which all such compendiums have, it does provide several useful pieces of information. It records the eighteenth-century preference for light-weight leather gloves, which were lined with fur for extra warmth; it mentions the other lines which nearly all glovers dealt in, and it describes the connection with breeches makers which was important throughout the century.

An apprenticeship to a glover would cost between £5 and £10, and when, after seven years, the young man had mastered the various aspects of his craft to the satisfaction of the Worshipful Company of Glovers who monitored the standards of gloving, he would either have to raise the necessary capital to set himself up as a master glover (anything between £50 and £500), or he would have to find work as a journeyman, someone who either was employed by a master, or travelled around the country in search of work.[5] There were few women master glovers; between 1788 and 1802 only six women became

2 Diderot's Encyclopédie, Tome IV, 1764. An English glovemaker's workshop would have been much like this one; all the necessary materials and equipment of their craft surround the two workers; the man in the background is assessing a skin before it is cut, whilst his companion is stitching a glove together.

members of the Glovers' Company, but female labour was widely recruited for the stitching of gloves.

The traditional methods of glovemaking are illustrated by the plates which accompanied the article on glovemaking in Diderot's *Encyclopédie*, published in 1764. It must be remembered that the French had a long, proud history of glovemaking, and this article records the best eighteenth-century practices. One illustration shows the glover's workshop with the master assessing the skin before cutting (fig. 2). His assistant or apprentice is stitching gloves, and they are both surrounded by the necessities of their craft: skins, shears, threads and in the right-hand corner,

near the fireplace there is a staking beam, so that the leather can be rendered more supple if required. Another illustration contains tools (fig. 3). Shown are the cutting shears and knife used by the glover for the different sections of a glove, and different weights of skin; the marble slab on which a skin was 'doled', using a sharp metal scraper which thinned the skin for particular parts of a glove; also illustrated are wood and marble weights, measures and gauges for the individual sizes and sections of a pair of gloves; and a staking beam.

There are two illustrations in the *Encyclopédie* which show the pieces of a glove after they have been cut out, and the different styles of gloves and mittens worn by men in the eighteenth century. A similar process was followed for women's gloves (these illustrations are reproduced in Chapter 3). Fig. 4 shows the main body of the glove, minus the thumb; the thumb and the quirk, a piece which fitted in at the base of the thumb; and the strengthening band placed inside the wrist. Fig. 5 shows the fourchettes, the side panels for the fingers; the gussets inserted at the junction of the fingers; the different finished

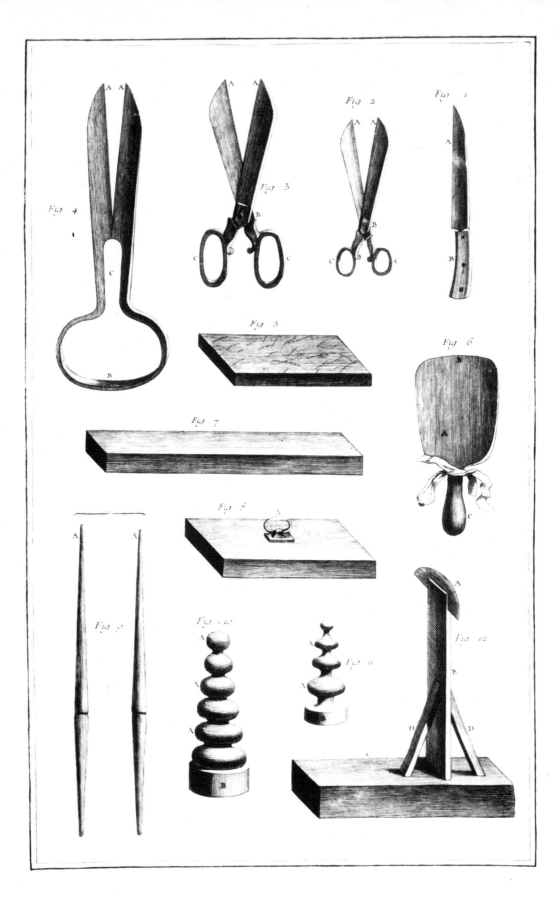

◁ 3 Diderot's Enclyclopédie, *Tome IV, 1764. Glove-making tools included shears and knife (items 1-4), a doling slab and knife (5 and 6), weights (7 and 8), gauges and measures (9-11), and a staking beam (12).*

gloves, ranging from as simple leather glove without a cuff to a glove with embroidery on the cuff and round the insertion of the thumb; and the shapes and the finished article when mittens rather' than gloves were wanted, when the process was much simpler and therefore less expensive. One common variant, not illustrated, was the top and palm sections of the hand cut separately.

The type of stitching used on the French examples was prix seam, stitches through the glove parallel to the edge. Thinner leather gloves were stitched by the round seam method, with the glove edges held back to back, and the stitching passing through, and over the edge of the seam. Details about stitching and embroidery at particular periods will be found in later chapters.

Even this brief introduction to the work of the glover will have shown that skill in assessing the fit of a glove, and its finish, were likely to vary from maker to maker. Not until the mid-nineteenth century did any major technical advances take place which could

4 Diderot's Encyclopédie, *Tome IV, 1764. Some of the various sections of men's gloves before they were stitched together: the hand (item 1), the thumb (2), the quirk (3) and the inside wrist band (4) (see the next illustration).*

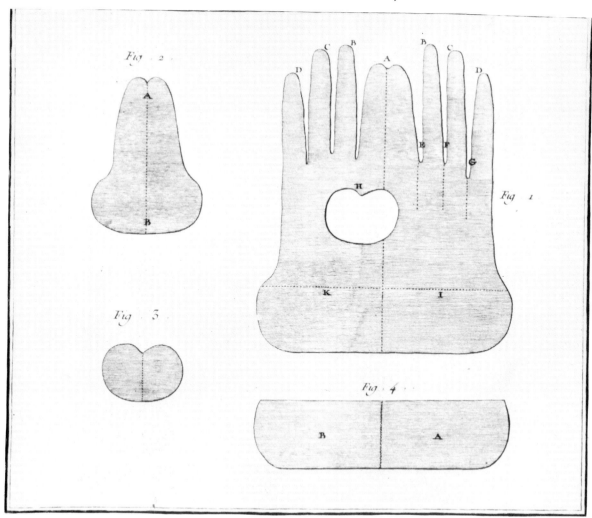

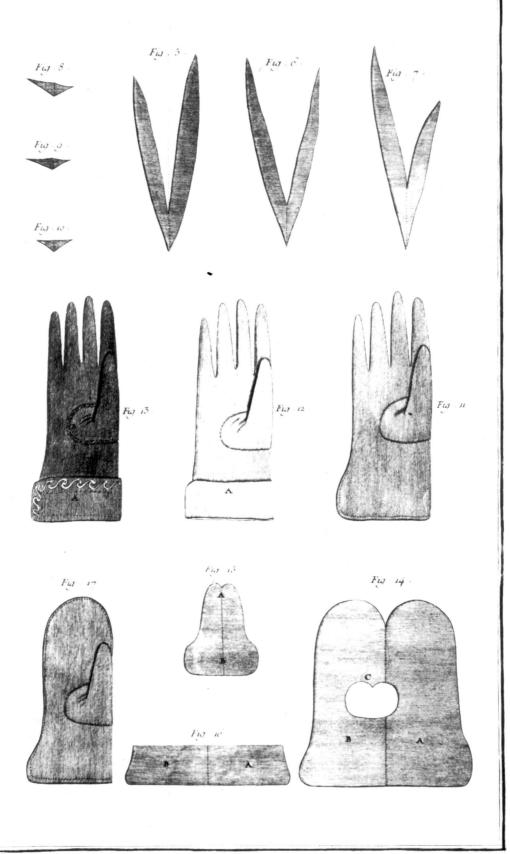

◁ 5 *Diderot's* Encyclopédie, *Tome IV, 1764. The remaining sections of men's gloves: the fourchettes (items 5-7) and gussets (8-10); three varieties of finished glove are illustrated in 11-13, and 14-17 show the construction of men's mittens.*

---

be considered as of lasting importance in improving the fit, finish and speed of production of gloves. The first innovation occurred in France when a glove manufacturer named Vallet d'Artois invented three sizes of steel punches which cut up to two dozen gloves per operation out of a pile of leather tranks (the amount of skin required for the main body of a glove).

In the eighteenth and nineteenth centuries there were a series of inventions in the textile industry and allied trades which mechanized many processes which had previously depended on the employment of large numbers of hand workers. Many of these advances were resisted, either by workers who were afraid of losing their livelihood, or by the master craftsmen who felt that no machine was capable of rivalling the skills and experience of trained workers. In the case of the invention by Vallet d'Artois the latter situation prevailed. It was a crude invention, in need of many refinements, but glove manufacturers chose to ignore it. It was left to Xavier Jouvin, a young French medical student who came from Grenoble, the centre of French glovemaking, to develop this idea. He studied the hands of patients in the hospital in Grenoble and eventually identified 320 sizes. Using this information he invented a glove pattern or calibre which he patented in 1834, and followed this with a punch for stamping out gloves, with separate dies for the smaller pieces like thumbs, fourchettes and gussets, and patented these in 1838. However, glove manufacturers in France were not impressed, and being businessmen as well as craftsmen they were most unwilling to pay to use this new system.

In 1839 the new system was awarded a bronze medal at the Industrial Exposition in Paris, and because Jouvin's patent only operated in France, the German, Swiss and Italian glove manufacturers who wanted to extend their markets, and could see the benefits of the system in terms of increased production, quickly introduced it into their workshops and factories. Only in 1849, when the patents lapsed in France, was Jouvin's system widely adopted in his native land, but international recognition came when he was awarded a diploma of honour at the Universal Exposition held in Vienna in 1851. All modern methods of glove sizing and pattern cutting are based on Jouvin's system.

The other major development which speeded up glove manufacture was the adaptation of the sewing machine to the finicky and specialized stitching required in the glove trade. One of the first machines appeared at the Paris Exposition of 1867, and although many gloves were hand stitched well into the twentieth century, and some types still are, glove stitching machinery gradually became accepted by all major manufacturing countries.

In discussing glove manufacturing as an industry it is important not to conjure up a picture of serried ranks of machinists in large factories. This happened in some countries, but the cottage industry element of glovemaking is retained to this day, and can be traced back to the earliest recorded makers. Although the preparation of the skins and the sorting, selecting and cutting of gloves was invariably centralized either in large or small yards, workshops and factories, many gloves were always placed in the hands of out-workers, usually women or girls. Even after the introduction of sewing machines, many glove manufacturers were willing to train their workers in the factories, and then allow them to have a machine in their own home once they left to marry or have children.

THE PRODUCTION OF FABRIC GLOVES

Gloves or mittens made of linen, silk or cotton and cut out and sewn in the manner of leather gloves, were not originally considered an adjunct of the glovemaking trade. In the seventeenth and eighteenth centuries they were usually made and supplied by the milliner or dressmaker. The word 'milliner' has changed its meaning in the last two hundred years, and today it is reserved to describe the makers of female head wear. In the seventeenth century it still retained its link with its origins, that is a trader in goods from Milan. These goods were an assortment of trimmings, buttons, braids and small accessories, which included fabric gloves.

The skills required were essentially dressmaking ones, and gloves or mittens made from fabric were often ordered or purchased because they complemented a particular dress, and because they were cooler and lighter to wear in warm weather or crowded rooms. Their major disadvantage was that they were rarely well fitting, and after one or two wearings they quickly lost their shape and any pretense of fit. However, their comparative cheapness ensured their place in fashionable dress, and at the end of the eighteenth century and beginning of the nineteenth century they were an appropriate accessory for the soft, gauzy fashions worn by women. The fabric glove industry was assisted in its growth by the technical advances made in textile machinery in the eighteenth century. Today fabric gloves are considered a separate category from knitted gloves, but the two areas overlapped considerably during the period 1770-1870. This was inevitable until the types of finish became noticeably different.

Framework knitted gloves and mittens were made in the Midlands of England, around Nottingham and Leicester primarily. The elasticity of these gloves made them popular, and they were knitted from both silk and cotton yarns. They lacked the smooth, tight, even gauge which characterized woven materials, and existed alongside gloves cut and stitched from silk, linen and cotton fabrics. As the knitted fabrics increased in sophistication, with the patenting of devices which could produce eyelet hole fabric (1764), figured lace web (1769), and twilled and patterned knitting (1776), the range out-stripped many conventional woven fabrics. A warp knitting machine, uniting the best principles of the loom and the stocking frame, was introduced in the mid-1770s, thus increasing further the range of patterns for both hosiery and other knitted items.[6]

The distinction between knitted and fabric gloves was blurred further by the growing practice of items being cut from a piece of knitted fabric and then sewn up, as opposed to being wrought and finished on the frame. In fact this practice was the fore-runner of the production techniques of the majority of nineteenth- and twentieth-century fabric glove manufacturers, but early in the nineteenth century efforts to prevent this method were attempted in a parliamentary bill of 1812 which sought means of, '. . . preventing frauds and abuses in framework knitting manufacture . . . .'[7] This caution was understandable, as framework knitters had not yet recognized the growing distiction between fabric gloves — knitted or otherwise — and genuine knitted gloves. However, at the time of its introduction the bill adversely affected the important trade in cotton gloves between England and North America. The change from wrought knitted gloves to cut-up gloves had reduced the price from 12 shillings to 5 shillings 9 pence per dozen pairs, thus increasing demand and benefitting manufacturers, exporters, importers and the American and Canadian shopkeepers.[8]

Warp knitting machines influenced all nineteenth- and twentieth-century developments in fabric glove-making, so the reader needs to understand the basic principles of this type of machine. In essence, warp knitting uses only vertical threads, completely omitting the weft threads which, on a loom, crossed and linked horizontally with the warp to produce a traditional woven fabric. The warp threads, carried on a beam and controlled by guide bars, were looped onto needles, and joined vertically. The end result was a stronger, more tightly knitted fabric than that produced on a knitting frame. Initially warp frames were used for lacemaking, and the production of fancy open work or lace effect gloves and mittens was a side line to this type of product.

However, in 1812 William Haimes of Melbourne in Derbyshire started making silk warp knitted gloves and mittens as his main trade, and his company went on to pioneer important new machinery for producing glove fabrics.[9] These warp knitted fabrics were cut out and sewn by hand, and it soon became obvious that unless the stitching was of the highest quality the gloves and mittens would give under the pressure of wear, and rip and unravel the fabric. In an attempt to solve this problem, Thomas Haimes patented a double needle bar machine in 1854 which produced seamless gloves. This machine was the earliest version of the later Simplex machine. Seamless gloves also have their disadvantages, particularly where fit is concerned, and by the 1850s the revolutionary new aid to tight, even stitching was on the horizon in the guise of the sewing machine, and by the late 1860s was in use for stitching gloves. Although the English invented machinery which produced a range of fabrics particularly suited to glovemaking, namely the Simplex and Milanese machines (the latter was developed in Derbyshire in the 1840s and went through various stages before being built for fabric production in Nottingham in 1880), it was the Germans who took the ideas, improved them, and went on to capture European markets in the post 1870 period.[10]

Three types of machinery were used to produce a stream of new fabrics and finishes for fabric gloves. The Milanese machine, used mainly to knit silk fabric, and much later rayon, had a different movement from other machines, and produced a fabric similar in appearance, but different in construction from the others. It was a slow machine, and by c.1900 the Germans were producing a similar fabric on a faster machine. The single bar warp knitting machine was used to knit lightweight cotton fabrics, and because the Germans used this machine to develop Atlas cloth, it is sometimes referred to as an Atlas machine. Atlas cloth was an imitation suede; the finish was obtained by passing the fabric over rollers covered with emery cloth. The Germans also experimented with pasting two pieces of Atlas cloth together to form a fabric which looked like chamois leather — this was known as Duplex cloth — but problems arose when the gloves were washed and the fabrics parted, and by c.1909 a Duplex fabric was being produced on a Simplex machine. This is a double bar machine which produced a double-faced fabric, and after dyeing and finishing, it closely resembled chamois leather or doeskin.

The endless experiments with finishing and dyeing in order to produce gloves which simulated their leather counterparts, but at much lower cost, was one of the most interesting features of the pre-1914 period. These gloves were also easier to care for, as they washed readily, and they gained an important share of the market throughout the world. Many leather glove manufacturers diversified to include these products in their ranges. This amalgamation was inevitable both for economic reasons, and also because the methods of cutting and stitching the fabric were so similar to those employed when making leather gloves.

In 1913 nine out of ten pairs of fabric gloves sold in Great Britain were German, and more than 100 million pairs of gloves were exported annually from Germany to the rest of the world before the First World War. When war started British manufacturers had to concentrate their energies on finding and developing fabrics to fill the void, and by 1920 they were producing 25 million pairs annually of suede Atlas, Duplex and Simplex gloves for the home market and for export.[11] Sadly this renaissance did not last long; Germany was soon underselling British products again, and by 1939, of the eighty glove manufacturers who had been in business in 1920, only six were left, producing just two million pairs annually.

In the 1930s Courtaulds pioneered a high speed warp knitting machine which was simpler in construction, and easier to operate than earlier models. It produced Atlas of locknit fabrics and, with adaptations, open work patterns, and it was soon copied in Europe and North America. During the Second World War there were experiments with nylon and spun rayon in an attempt to overcome the cotton shortage, and these developments continued into peacetime. Today the majority of fabric gloves are made from artificial fibres, mainly nylon, and the bulk of them are imported from continental Europe and the Far East.

THE PRODUCTION OF KNITTED GLOVES

We have seen how difficult it was in the eighteenth and nineteenth centuries to draw a firm distinction between machine-knitted gloves and gloves made from a knitted fabric. However, long before the invention of the knitting frame, and long afterwards, knitted gloves were a useful, but inexpensive accessory for the poorer classes in society. Until fairly recently, hand-knitted gloves have never enjoyed much in the way of public esteem. In his book on gloves, B.E. Ellis writing in 1921, states unequivocally, 'The improvement in manufacturing processes, leading to rapid and cheap production of these goods, has been of particular benefit to the working classes, providing them with serviceable hand-wear at a price well within reach of the poorest.'[12]

Knitted gloves, to this day, are considered the practical and unglamourous end of the market, although those readers who are familiar with the beautifully patterned and richly coloured Spanish and Italian silk gloves and mittens which were knitted for both the Catholic clergy and rich laity may dispute this statement. In England, however, knitted gloves were usually fairly utilitarian. The constant and abundant supply of wool made it the most natural medium for hand knitting, although, as we have already seen, frame-knitted gloves were often made of cotton and silk as well.

Hand knitting continued alongside frame knitting as a craft industry until the early nineteenth century. In 1774, when Postlethwayte published his *Dictionary of Trade and Commerce*, he mentioned that Doncaster had a thriving trade in hand-knitted gloves, stockings, waistcoats and petticoats, whilst Christchurch in Hampshire had, as its principal manufacture, gloves and stockings.[13] In other European countries the production of hand-knitted items lasted, as a craft industry, well into the nineteenth century, because import duties levied on foreign machine-knitted products made them more expensive than hand-knitted native items.[14]

Gradually hand-knitting diminished into a domestic craft, although in certain parts of the country hand workers continued to knit their handsome, specialized designs which owed much of their charm to the fact that no two items were ever quite identical (fig. 6). In terms of production numbers and regularity of finish, however, machine-knitted items were preferred in the nineteenth and twentieth centuries, except in the brief periods when 'natural' fashions enjoyed public acclaim.

In essence there were two types of knitted gloves, seamless and wrought. The first type were produced partly on circular hosiery machines and partly on flat hand-knitting machines. Wrought gloves, which allowed a wider variety of stitches and patterns to be

used, were fashioned in shaped parts with a selvage, and the parts were seamed together on a sewing machine designed for joining hosiery. Many hosiery manufacturers produced gloves as a natural adjunct to their other products.

Today, many knitted gloves, made from wool, synthetic fibres or a mixture of both, are in great demand because they are both cheap and warm. Japanese machines can produce a finished, seamless glove with an elasticated wrist every two-and-a-half minutes, and up to six or eight of these machines can be minded by one worker. No other type of glove can hope to compete with this level of production.

2

'Rich Embroidered Gloves'
1600-1699

When James I visited Oxford University in 1605, the university authorities presented him with a pair of gloves 'the turnover [cuff or gauntlet] wrought with purl'[1] which cost them £6. Ten years later when Cambridge University was honoured by a royal visit the king was presented with 'a fair pair of perfumed gloves with gold laces'.[2] Gloves were an acceptable and costly gift in the seventeenth century, and the tradition of presenting distinguished visitors, patrons or friends with beautiful, if impractical gloves, was long established. The lists of New Year gifts presented to Queen Elizabeth I always contain two or three pairs of gloves. Such gifts were both visually appealing and symbolically significant, demonstrating loyalty and service to the recipient.

Many items of clothing that today are considered functional or essential for warmth and comfort were charged with symbolism, which in the seventeenth century was understood perfectly. In different circumstances they could represent a legal contract, a form of peppercorn rent, a reward for service or a form of supplication for expected favours. They were presented to wedding guests or provided for funeral attire, or in happier circumstances they were a sign of courtesy and friendship.[3] The survival in public and private collections of so many fine examples of seventeenth-century gloves is due in part to the fact that there was an acknowledged difference between gloves which were worn as practical accessories and those which were so splendidly decorated that they constituted acceptable, but impractical presents. This is not to imply that they were never worn; many of them almost certainly found their way onto the hands of their owners on a few occasions, but they were not 'wearing' gloves, and therefore did not wear out.

In British portraiture in the first half of the seventeenth century, there are very few examples of sitters wearing or holding the types of glove which, in museum collections, are considered typical of the prevalent style of that period. Such portraits draw our attention to the wide gulf which generally exists between gloves which were worn and gloves which survive. Certainly in the first twenty years of the century the clothes of both men and women were flamboyant, richly decorated with embroidery, lace and braid, a demonstrable sign of a prevailing desire in society to show status and wealth in expensive forms of dress. Yet even royal sitters wear the simpler varieties of glove, plain, natural coloured leather with no decoration or just a hint of applied braid or outline embroidery. Ironically, it was the sturdy, God-fearing and upright Flemish and Dutch citizens, the majority of whom were what might loosely be termed middle-class in today's language, who held or wore the styles of glove which we identify today as early seventeenth century. In the portrait of a family by Cornelis de Vos (Museum voor Schone Kunsten, Ghent), painted 1635-40 the richly embroidered gloves held by the woman are in stark contrast to the sombre black of her dress. The vibrant pinks of the threads and ribbon are an exact parallel to the gloves one finds in British collections.

Obviously gloves were not restricted to any one class in society, and throughout the centuries the restrictions on the wearing of certain fashions are a good indication of how easy it was for people to ape their betters. During James I's reign there were a series of prohibitions on certain types of fashionable accessory. Apprentices, for example, were forbidden to wear gloves which cost more than 1 shilling a pair, or gloves with fingers or trimmings which consisted of gold or silver lace, velvet or silk lace or ribbons.[4] In effect they were being reduced to the simplest leather or woollen mittens, which would have cost something like 3 or 4 pence a pair. Whether these prohibitions were much regarded must be in some doubt as an Italian visitor to England in 1618 noticed that in London 'all wear very costly gloves. The fashion of gloves is so universal that even the porters wear them very ostentatiously.'[5]

The gloves which were available in such profusion fell into various categories. The plainest leather, wool and linen gloves and mittens have not survived, but were certainly of British manufacture. The importation of gloves into England had been prohibited in 1463, but foreign visitors and English travellers brought European gloves into the country from time to time, although these were more likely to have been richly decorated examples rather than the plainer varieties.

However, as already mentioned, it is the plainer gloves which appear most frequently in contemporary portraits. They were worn by both men and women, and were usually made of soft, neutral-coloured leather, with a short, turnover cuff, often white, but sometimes coloured (fig. 7). In the Wardrobe Account for 1608 of Prince Henry of Wales, thirty-one pairs of gloves are listed. The majority of these were quite plain, and included 'Six pair plain gloves with coloured tops, and some white tops'.[6] These cost 3 shillings per pair and are the sort seen in the portraits of the time.

Plain gloves were traditional wedding favours for guests. In *The Silent Woman* (1609), one of Ben Jonson's characters says, 'We see no ensign of a wedding here, no character of a bridale — Where be our scarves and our gloves'.[7] Two years later, a bridegroom, commenting on purchases in connection with his own wedding, wrote, 'I could not get so many woman's Jessamy gloves as [I] wrote for; and at the last was fained to pick upon cordient for men and perfumed kid for women. I had them perfumed better than ordinary that they might give content.'[8] Perfumed gloves were an extra expense, and a bridegroom could run up a steep bill if his wedding was well attended.

The glover often acted as perfumer, although it was possible for the parsimonious to buy perfume and scent the gloves themselves. Charles I bought his gloves from Joseph Atkinson and Robert Hutchinson in the mid-1630s, and the latter was also a perfumer who provided this service for other items of clothing apart from gloves, using 'muske, Civet, Amber and spirit of Roses'.[9] Atkinson also dealt in other wares, providing the king with such accessories as girdles, belts and sword hangers. The provision of perfume or small items made of leather was not unusual for glovemakers, as the two forms of business were either inter-related — the glovers of Paris were described as marchands-maîtres-gantiers-parfumeurs[10] — or they were extensions of the craft itself, the preparation of items from leather.

Although plain gloves were a regular and profitable line, both as everyday items in the wardrobe of men and women, and as an expected form of wedding gift or favour, they are not the gloves which interest the connoisseur today. What attracts attention and admiration are the splendidly embroidered gloves of the first half of the seventeenth century (plates 1 and 2). These gloves, many of which survive in collections throughout Europe and North America, are, in their finest form, small elegant works of art, a perfect amalgam of the two crafts of glovemaking and embroidery. It seems probable that the fashionable glover employed or contracted his work to one or more embroiderers. Some gloves could easily be assembled from the two component parts: the glove and the embroidered gauntlet, separately executed and united when each section was nearly finished. Other examples, in which the embroidery was worked directly onto a one-piece gauntlet glove, obviously required consecutive rather than simultaneous processes.

When confronted with the various styles of early seventeenth-century gloves, it is not always easy to determine whether they were all fashionable at approximately the same time, varying in style and decoration according to the tastes of their original owners, or whether they represent a sequence of styles, often overlapping, but demonstrating subtle changes in fashion. If they are considered in relationship to the portraits of the time, the latter is more probable.

Before considering the various styles of embroidered gloves, it is useful to know something about their structure and appearance. All of them, whether wholly made of leather or with a gauntlet of different material, were usually made of dressed lamb or doeskin with a soft, natural finish similar to suede, and the most elegant examples are off-white or pale golden tan, although grey and a darker tan were also worn. The glover selected, cut and supervised the stitching of the glove in the traditional manner (see Chapter 1) according to the size required by the customer. There seems to have been a simple sizing system which coped with all but the narrowest and widest hands, as the majority of surviving gloves measure 9 or 9.5 cm across the knuckles, although in rare instances a glove with a measurement as small as 7.5 cm can be found. Determining the sex of the original wearer of early seventeenth-century gloves is always a speculative rather than an exact affair unless

---

7 Lady Scudamore, by Marcus Gheeraedts the Younger, 1614-15. The plain buff leather gloves with white tops contrast sharply with the other items of dress which rely for their impact on complicated patterns and applied decoration. ▷

the gloves have an impeccable provenance. However, if the length and breadth of the hands are shorter and narrower by up to 2 cm than other examples, it is usually fair to assume that the wearer was a woman. All of the gloves seem to have excessively long fingers, and lines of wear indicate that the finger tips rarely extended the last 1½-2 cm to the tips of the gloves.

This curious feature cannot be explained as being inaccurate measurements by the glover, as the elongated effect also extended into the upper half of the glove. The stitching of each finger and fourchette is extended as far as the knuckles, sometimes using silver gilt or coloured silk threads to emphasize this feature (plate 2). Although the origins of some fashions are difficult to trace, it is possible that Elizabeth I may have influenced this one. She was excessively proud of her long, narrow fingered hands, and although not a tall woman (she was perhaps 5 foot 4 inches or 5 foot 5 inches in height) the gloves she left at Oxford University (now in the collection of the Ashmolean Museum) are extraordinarily long, with a middle finger measurement of 12 cm, although they measure only 8.5 cm across the knuckles. These gloves were a presentation pair, but it is unlikely that they were commissioned without due regard to the queen's known preferences. Such gloves are, like the seventeenth-century examples, signs of splendid in-activity. They are an unsubtle sign of prestige; a sign of the presence of servants who would do all the

necessary awkward handling and carrying, leaving their masters and mistresses free to look elegant and unencumbered. For more active pursuits, like riding, hawking, or on more mundane occasions, gloves were either decorated very simply, or plain, and as the century progressed and fashions became more restrained, gloves followed suit.

The gauntlets, whether in one piece with the glove or separately executed items, had an inner, half lining of silk to mask the back of the embroidery stitches. If the embroidery was worked onto a satin or silk ground it was usually backed with canvas to support the material. When the embroidery was particularly heavy an additional layer of stiffened paper or card was placed between the ground and the lining to prevent the gauntlet from buckling. The line where the gauntlet and glove were joined was usually masked by a band of ruched silk ribbon or a line of silver gilt or gold lace. Often the embroidery was edged with metal lace or fringe, with spangles scattered amongst the trimming.

---

8 Glove, 1600-1610. Cream doeskin with the glove and gauntlet stitched together at the wrist; the embroidery design of stylized carnations and leaves is executed in gold thread and yellow silk; the fringe is silver gilt, trimmed with spangles.

Amongst the earliest examples are leather gauntlet gloves treated in two sections and stitched together at the wrist (fig. 8). The embroidery design usually consisted of a formal pattern of flowers within borders or arches worked in coloured silks and metal threads. This style can be recognized by the charming complementary bands of embroidery worked around the thumb; and by the side gusset bands which are always leather rather than silk. The disadvantage of the embroidery around the thumb, attractive though it is as a design feature, is that it rubbed too easily. These gloves were derived in style from the presentation pair given to Elizabeth I when she visited Oxford in 1566, and the later versions probably date from the turn of the century, 1595-1610.

The gloves discussed above survive in comparatively small numbers, and are outstripped numerically by the one-piece gauntlet glove. The most lavishly decorated examples use the whole of the gauntlet for tightly constructed embroideries in which metal thread predominated, highlighted by some coloured silks. The designs were carefully formulated to produce a symmetrical but variable line between the embroidery and leather at the wrist edge (fig. 9). The motifs used for the embroidery are similar to those found on other gloves and are discussed later in this chapter. These highly decorated versions were probably fashionable until the mid-1630s.

9 Glove, 1615-25. Cream leather one-piece glove embroidered with gold and silver threads, and edged with a matching fringe attached to a pink silk braid; the design incorporates both mythical and known beasts.

For the sake of clarity, it is easiest to divide the other styles, with separate gauntlets of material other than leather, into four types. Type one had a band of material wider at the upper edge than at the wrist join, with an oblique angle on the outside edge of the gauntlet. The second type was a variation of this style, with a stepped edge between gauntlet and glove (plate 2). The third variety had a gauntlet consisting of six to eight tabs or waisted panels with round top edges, and the fourth variety usually had six angular tabs with straight top edges (fig. 10). An embryonic form of both of these last two styles developed in the 1580s, and was still found in the early years of the seventeenth century, up to c.1610. These earlier gloves had shallow tabs at the top of a plain gauntlet, either rounded or squared off (plate 1).

All of the gauntlet styles are either open at the outside edge of the gauntlet, or they have small gussets of silk or narrow openings between the tabs (plate 2). Those with a side opening usually have two

*10 Gloves, 1610-30. Cream leather glove with dark
blue satin round tabs, embroidered alternately with
bunches of grapes and the pelican in her peity within
scroll and serpentine traceries, using gold thread, seed
pearls and coloured silks; ruched pink silk band and
gold and silver lace. Buff leather glove with squared
tabs embroidered alternately with carnations and
roses with a pelican in her piety at the base, using
couched pink cord, laid gold thread, seed pearls and
spangles; wrist band of pink silk, gold lace and
spangles.*

or three narrow horizontal ribbons which act as a
type of decorative gusset. Both forms of gusset helped
to prevent the sleeve and cuffs being crushed or dis-
torted by the gloves.

The earliest types of gloves, those with abbreviated
tabs, worn from the late sixteenth century up until
c.1610, are usually embroidered in two or three
horizontal bands of decoration, on a plain satin
ground. The rows of embroidery often seem
unrelated, perhaps flowers in one band — often roses,
pansies or carnations — then a band with birds and
beasts or crude human figures in a fantastic,
imaginery landscape, all enclosed by smaller flowers,
leaves, fruits or sinuous scroll work (plate 1). Every
available inch of space is crammed with pattern,
worked in clear, rich blue, pink, green, red, purple,
yellow and brown silks, sometimes interspersed with
spangles or highlighted with silver gilt or gold threads.

The later round-tabbed varieties have much more
structured lines, and they obviously presented a particular design problem to the embroiderer, which was
solved altogether more elegantly. Each tab is usually

treated as a small embroidery in it own right, with formal, vertical lines of pattern which contrast with or echo the adjacent tab. The square-edged tabbed gauntlets often show a motif in the central area of the gauntlet which flows upwards and outwards to form a harmonious whole (fig. 10). Some of the loveliest examples contain quantities of seed pearls, coloured silk thread, gold thread and trimmings of gold bobbin lace decorated with spangles. Several versions of one design survive in different collections, indicating that the embroidery was probably a favourite design at a particular time. Although we tend to think of these gloves as small, individual pieces, worked to the specification of one customer, there was considerable repetition of certain groups of designs. However, there is evidence of specially commissioned work in the inventory of Richard Sackville, Earl of Dorset's wardrobe which was prepared in 1617-19, where each outfit of clothes had its own individual gloves to match, for instance, 'Item one paire of gloves with topps of cloth of silver embroadered with globes flames and hartes of gold and laced with small gold lace'.[11] Eight pairs of gloves are listed; they are all different and each pair is related to a specific outfit of clothes.

11 Gloves, 1620-35. Cream leather glove and white satin square tabbed gauntlet; each of the twelve tabs is embroidered with a different Arcadian scene within an oval surrounded by flowers and foliage, using polychrome silks, edged with silver gilt lace and spangles.

Tabbed gloves were probably most fashionable between 1610 and 1630. The early seventeenth-century flamboyance in dress extended until the mid-1620s, but it was at its apogee in the mid to late teens, 1614-19 when the Earl of Dorset is recorded as owning such individualistic pairs of gloves. The surviving portraits show figures dressed in highly decorated clothing with every available inch of surface covered with pattern, embroidery, braid, lace and jewellery, and many of the gloves reflect this delight in exuberant decoration.

Gradually the embroidery became more sophisticated, and the brilliance of seed pearls and the three dimensional qualities of the small figures, flora and fauna were replaced by a skilful use of flowers and cartouches containing stylized figures, executed in

smooth satin stitches in subtle colour mixtures, high-lighted by a discreet use of metal strip, couched, basket woven, and as fine thread, within a framework of curving lines and small flower motifs which mirror the sprig and lozenge designs found on woven silks at this date (fig. 11).

The other types of gauntlet gloves, with plain edges obliquely angled to the narrow wrist of the glove, and the allied stepped versions of this gauntlet, have many characteristics in common with the tabbed varieties. They too were densely embroidered with naturalistic motifs; flowers, birds, and beasts, and there was the same lavish use of seed pearls, metal strip and thread, and lace trimming decorated with spangles. The only real difference is one of degree. the shape of this type of gauntlet allowed for a symmetry of design without too much difficulty, and there are fewer examples of uneasy or irregular patterns (plate 2).

The embroidery on gloves echoes other seven-teenth-century embroideries (fig. 12), and drew upon similar sources for inspiration — illustrated

designs were executed for rich customers in a seemingly endless stream. However, the actual glovemaking element is not what we recall when thinking of these gloves; it is the skilful and costly embroidery, and although the glover would have taken his commission on the finished product, the most expensive and admired components were the silks, metal thread, braid and lace. The end result was a shared triumph, and like all fashionable triumphs it was ephemeral. The glovers and embroiderers moved onto different work, coming together occasionally for specialized items.

By the late 1620s and early 1630s we are able to refer to an interesting group of portraits which indicate how fashions changed according to the age and prominence of the sitter. A portrait of Richard Tomlins (now in the Bodleian Library, Oxford) shows a man of 64 holding a pair of densely embroidered and heavily fringed gloves. His contemporary, Sir Nicholas Bacon, painted at much the same time, is holding gauntlet gloves which are similarly fringed but which are decorated with four bands of applied metal braid. The young, saturnine Duke of Hamilton, painted wearing the height of fashion in 1629, wears gloves trimmed with only a narrow metal braid and fringe around the outside edges. A slightly older, but equally fashionable courtier, Henry Rich, Earl of Holland, painted c.1632, wears gloves somewhat similar in style to those carried by Nicholas Bacon six or seven years earlier, except the earl's are trimmed with five rows of metal braid, and are edged with short, bushy fringe (fig. 13).

From this visual evidence, I think that it is reasonable to deduce that by the late 1620s and early 1630s gloves for the younger or more worldly men were much plainer. Gauntlet gloves of leather were an ideal complement to soft knee-length boots and the plainer, less flamboyant fashions of Charles I's Court, but only if their decoration was similarly elegant and restrained. Obviously, the more formal varieties were still being produced, for gifts, but gloves gradually fell into line with the prevalent desire for an accessory which was both elegant and functional. Heavily decorated gloves looked anachronistic with the more restrained styles, and no craftsman was foolish enough to try and perpetuate a style for which demand was diminishing.

herbals and bestiaries, and the embroidery pattern books which reinterpreted these subjects for the professional embroiderer or the amateur needlewoman. There are some stylized features, the use of sinuous lines or lozenges to contain the design, but there was also a great demand for birds, beasts, fruits, flowers and human figures, all placed in a curious, almost surrealistic background of spangles, beads and coils of metal thread.

It is tempting to speculate that this was the heyday of the glover's art, when specially commissioned

Henry Rich Earl of
Holland.

◁ *13 Henry Rich, Earl of Holland, by Daniel Mytens, c. 1632. The simpler, more sculptural lines of the earl's dress are complemented by plainer accessories; the braided gloves echo the decoration on his doublet and breeches.*

Many of these simpler gloves survive; parallels can be found to the gloves worn by Nicholas Bacon, the Duke of Hamilton and the Earl of Holland (fig. 14). These are the gloves which were worn in the 1630s and 1640s. The decoration is discreet, perhaps a simple band of embroidery around the outside edge of the gauntlet, or narrow outline motifs, often roughly triangular in shape, which were less naturalistic, but simpler and less dominant. These are the types of gloves which Charles I purchased in such large quantities. Between September 1633 and September 1634 he paid £119 1 shilling to Joseph Atkinson, a sum which covered sword hangers, girdles etc. but also covered '37 dozen and 3 pairs of upper and under gloves; 2 dozen pairs of thick stags leather gloves with gold and silver frindges; 2 pairs of gloves trimmed with black tops for mourning . . . .'[12] These descriptions are of gloves which were much plainer than would have been expected ten years earlier. Fringed tops feature a good deal in these orders and describe the simpler gauntlet gloves of the 1630s on

which this decoration was a usual feature. During the years 1633-5 the king also bought '4 dozen of right handed gloves to shoote in . . .', '8 dozen pairs of Kidds leather gloves', but only '1 pair of rich embroidered gloves'.[13]

By the late 1640s we reach a watershed in the development and design of gloves. Men were wearing simpler, less ostentatious gloves to harmonize with their more sombre clothes. Women, wearing dresses with shorter sleeves, from the mid-1630s onwards, started to favour longer, plainer gloves cut to fit sleekly up to the elbow. During the Civil War and the Commonwealth period the pendulum of fashion swung further in the direction of simplicity, prompted by the Puritan distaste for fashionable novelties. Sombre clothes were the order of the day, and gloves, to judge from portraits and engravings, were plain, adorned, if at all, with narrow bands of gold lace or fringe. The relaxation that occurred with the Restoration of the monarchy in 1660 produced a new phase in glove design.

---

14 Glove, 1630-40. Mid-brown leather decorated with applied bands of pale blue satin ribbon overlaid with gold and silver gilt thread, and trimmed with silver gilt lace and spangles and a silver gilt fringe; this glove is similar to those worn by the Earl of Holland (13).

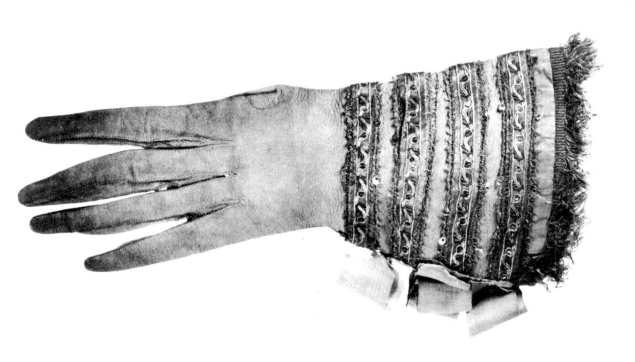

Men's gloves, as we have seen earlier, followed a different path from women's gloves from about the late 1630s onwards. This distinction continued for the rest of the century, except in the case of outdoor pursuits like riding or hunting. Women's gloves were always longer and more closely fitted to the arm. Men's gloves from about 1660 to the early 1670s reflected the fashionable interest in surface decoration which was characterized by an excessive use of looped ribbons (fig. 15). These gloves were much shorter than before, usually wrist length, with a shallow cuff, in white leather, pale buff or the rich cinnamon brown which was a favourite. Sadly, the passage of the centuries has diminished much of their original delicate charm. The looped and ruched ribbons which were applied to the cuff and back are faded and flattened, the soft, vivid pinks, greens, blues and silvers are uniformly subdued. They were very much gloves of the hour, not designed to withstand several centuries of retention in trunks, attics and cellars. Most accessories, at their finest and most

15 Men's gloves, 1660-80. All three gloves show the three-dimensional ruched and looped decoration found on gloves after the Restoration: mushroom doeskin with ribbons of green, blue, cream and silver tinsel round the wrist and down the outside hand; white leather with silver, white and orange ribbons trimmed with silver gilt fringe; white doeskin decorated with pinking and interwoven ribbons, and rosettes of pale and dark green silk.

original, are amusing novelties, existing as a temporary distraction alongside their plainer, more functional, workaday cousins. One such pair, in the Spence Collection of the Worshipful Company of Glovers, is still a delightful reminder of the frivolous 1660s. Made from short white leather, probably doeskin, with green stitching outlining the fingers and thumb, and with punched decoration on the glove, the cuff which is serrated at the join is laced with two bands of green ribbon woven through the slashed leather, and with two extra bands of ruched ribbon applied below each laced row. The hand of the glove was given a lively, three-dimensional quality by the use of ribbon rosettes, one on the centre back of the hand, and three, diminishing in size, applied down the length of the little finger (fig.15).

Samuel Pepys, whose interest in fashion was as whole-hearted as his many other preoccupations, was often at 'the New Exchange to buy gloves & other little errands'.[14] We have already encountered his annoyance, in Chapter 1, about Sir G. Downing's

gloves costing half the price of his own, although they were 'as handsome, as good in all points'.[15] When his father died in 1667 he 'resolved to put myself and wife, and Barker & Jane, W. Hewers and Tom in mourning, and my two undermaids, to give them hoods and scarfs & gloves'.[16] Thus custom of supplying mourners, including servants, and wedding guests with gloves, continued unabated. In 1685, Sir Ralph Verney records the largesse which accompanied Sir Richard Piggott's funeral, 'wee that bore up the pall had Rings, Scarfs, Hat-bands, Shammee Gloves of the best fashion . . . the rest of the Gentry had Rings and all the Servants Gloves . . . .'[17] The quantities of

16 'The Royal Exchange', by Wenceslas Hollar, c. 1648. This engraving of one of the fashionable London shopping areas shows the small specialist shops in which fashionable materials and accessories could be commissioned and purchased.

gloves involved in this type of gesture could be quite prodigious. Sir Walter Calverley, a Yorkshire gentleman, gave 140 pairs of gloves to the mourners and their servants at his sister's funeral in 1705.[18]

This was the sort of custom, coupled with the fashionable demand for new styles, which kept the glovers in business. At the opposite end of the spectrum was a frugal spender like Sarah Fell of Swarthmoor Hall whose household account books record a payment of 2 pennies to a local youth who mended four pairs of her sister's gloves.

This was in 1673, and in the same year she recorded other expenditure on the repair of gloves, the dyeing of gloves at 1 penny, and occasionally on the purchase of new gloves. Hedging and garden mittens figure largely, at a cost of 10 pence a pair. Her most expensive purchase was when she paid 'Mary Rigby for a p. of white cotton gloves for sistr. Rachell 0.2.0 '.[19] People like Sarah Fell probably bought their sturdy hedging and garden mittens from local skindressers who made the simpler types of glove or mitten as an adjunct to their main business, or from pedlars, local fairs or markets. Mary Rigby who provided cotton gloves was possibly a local dressmaker or milliner who acquired her stock at the large markets which sold to tradespeople and individuals. Retailing outside the larger towns was an uncertain affair in the seventeenth century, and the wealthier courtry-based customer usually sent to the nearest large town or to London for goods of this type (fig.16).

17 Men's gloves, 1680-1700. Buff-coloured leather riding gloves embroidered with silver gilt thread and edged with a deep bullion fringe interspersed with metal coils and tassels.

18 Queen Mary II, c. 1690. The gloves worn by the ▷ queen are a representative pair of the plainer sort of elbow length gloves worn by fashionable women in the late 17th century.

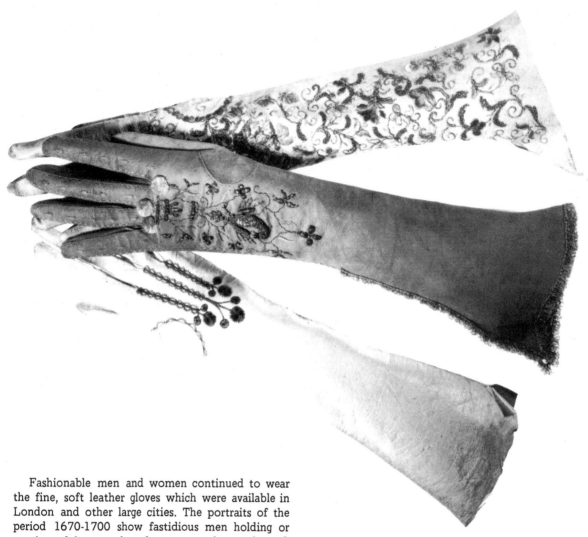

Fashionable men and women continued to wear the fine, soft leather gloves which were available in London and other large cities. The portraits of the period 1670-1700 show fastidious men holding or wearing plain gauntlet gloves, sometimes trimmed with a discreet band of gold or silver braid or a heavy fringe. Occasionally the exquisite might, at the risk of derision, wear gloves similar to those worn by women. The playwright Etherege, in *The Man of Mode*, written in 1676, describes one character: 'He is indeed a pattern of modern foppery. He was yesterday at the Play, with a Pair of Gloves up to his elbows.'[20] This was rare, the most noticeable men's gloves in the 1680s and 1690s were heavy, much-decorated official-looking gauntlets. Two pairs of these survive in the Spence Collection. Both pairs are wide, with a curving outer edge. The backs of each hand are embroidered with stylized vertical bands of silver gilt thread, but it is the fringing around the top and side edge of the gauntlets which catches the eye.

19 *Women's gloves, 1685-1700. Suede leather elbow-length gloves came in a wide range of colours, from palest creams and whites to dark rich blues and greens; they were embroidered with serpentine trails of flowers and birds in polychrome silks, or subtly highlighted by rows of contrast pointing on the back of the hand.*

The heavy silver gilt fringe is interspersed with massive, intricately coiled bullion tassels (fig. 17). The combined weight of this decoration must have been most uncomfortable for the wearer, but oviously provided a magnificent spectacle for the onlooker, because the fringe falls naturally in an elegant curving line onto the hand of the glove. These specimens were probably the last of the elegant but impractical presentation gloves which were such a feature of seventeenth-century glovemaking. A more wearable version of such gloves survive in a private collection. They were worn by a Gentleman of the Bedchamber to William III. They are tan leather lined with blue silk, with a plain silver gilt fringe falling from a narrow woven braid. A bill for a similar pair of fringed gloves is found among the Verney Papers, and reads,

For A Payre of orangery Gloves   £1 1s 6d
For A Scarletit gold and Silluer fringe
   to trimme them   £5 0 0
For Faceing to them and fringing them £0 5 6 [21]

Women's gloves at the end of the century blossomed into a range of lovely colours, pink, blue, green, cinnamon, white and natural. They were elbow-length, curving outwards at the upper edge, often fairly plain with decorative stitching on the fingers and around the thumb, with elegant rows of pointing on the back of the hand (fig. 18). Some pairs are edged with feather silk fringe or have small silk tufts on the backs of the hand just on the knuckle line (fig. 19). Some versions of these gloves have small groups of flowers embroidered on the back of the glove, others have birds or figures, and in the last category there is a surviving pair, in the Spence Collection, which provides a dating key to this fashion. The pair of gloves, of cinnamon leather with blue silk tassels across the knuckles, has a meandering design of flowers worked from a band at the top of the glove down the outside arm and around a small female figure on the back of the hand. This figure, although primitive in its design, is unmistakeably wearing the fashions of the 1690s. Another pair is embroidered from the silk tassels on the knuckles to the top edge of the gloves with a swirling design of flowers and leaves, creating the impression of two delicate but vivid flower gardens on a miniature scale.

3

Formal Simplicity
1700-1799

After the delights of seventeenth-century gloves, both male and female, the eighteenth century provides a rather inspid range. Curiously it is the century when gloves for women, and to a lesser extent men, became an indispensable accessory, and not just for the constant round of weddings and funerals which provided such a useful boost to the glove sellers. By 1734 these comments can be found in Henry Fielding's *The Universal Gallant*: ' . . . I never gave my hand to any man without a glove' and 'the first time a woman's hand should be touched is in church'.[1] Although the reticence among women may seem absurd, it was not the major reason for their universal wearing of gloves. In practical terms, they reaffirmed all of the seventeenth-century preoccupations with inactivity and social status, and expressed a new worry, protecting the arms from sunshine. While a bronzed skin might seem healthy and pleasing in a bucolic peasant, it was not appreciated in a well brought up young woman. However, as anyone who has tried to handle fine items while wearing gloves knows there is a considerable loss of tactile sense even when wearing the lightest ones. Not that every sort of activity during waking hours was carried out wearing gloves. At the dinner table gloves were removed, as we can tell by the remarks in Samuel Richardson's novel *Pamela*, written in 1740, when Mr B. says, 'Let us go in to dinner, come my young lady, shall I help you off with your white gloves?'[2]

A novel, although rather curious solution to this problem is found in the fashion for gloves with open fingertips. A reference in 1740 to 'fine white thread gloves that are open-fingered'[3] can be matched by the later illustrations to the entry in Diderot's *Encyclopédie* (figs. 20 and 21). These illustrations show the basic construction of women's gloves and mittens in the eighteenth century, and include a pair of gloves with open fingertips, though in this instance they were made of leather.

Although women's gloves in the eighteenth century seem of more interest than men's, in the first half of the century men's gloves were still a prominent accessory, although sadly there are few surviving examples. Gauntlet gloves were worn as fashionable accessories until c.1750, but by 1753 a contemporary commentator was writing, 'who dare appear now in high-topped gloves?'[4] Plain gauntlets were worn for riding much later than this, but by the 1740s no men with pretensions to elegance would have appeared in a fashionable centre wearing such gloves. These early eighteenth-century high-topped gloves were often trimmed with a narrow band of metal braid, or edged with fringe. Defoe described one character in *Moll Flanders* as wearing a 'full bottomed wig and silver-fringed gloves'.[5]

The shorter, wrist-length gloves, completely plain, or with a narrow cuff, sometimes decorated with a discreet drizzle of embroidery, were worn from the early years of the century as an alternative to gauntlet gloves, and gradually displaced them as the fashionable length of town wear. Such gloves were made from a variety of leathers, usually in a natural buff or light tan shade.

It is possible, by examining the work of just one portrait painter, Thomas Gainsborough, to be convinced of the great simplicity of men's gloves in the post-1740 period. Gainsborough's sitters ranged from country gentry to royalty, and those depicted wearing or holding gloves, from Robert Andrews in the double portrait of 1748 (fig. 22), to George Drummond in 1780 (fig. 23), all favoured the plainest, natural-coloured gloves. Some pairs were a little longer than others and settled into soft creases just above the wrist (fig. 22), others had three decisive lines of pointing on the back of the hand

---

20 Diderot's Encyclopédie, *Tome IV, 1764. Items* ▷ *18-28 show the sections which were cut out and stitched together to produce medium length, loose fitting women's gloves; 29 illustrates a longer, closer fitting glove of the open fingered variety (see fig. 21).*

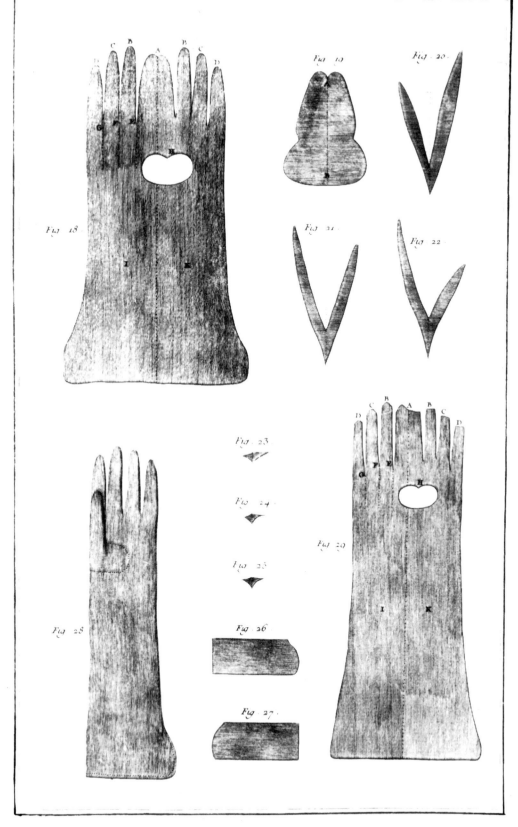

Fig. 18.

Fig. 19.

Fig. 20.

Fig. 21.

Fig. 22.

Fig. 23.

Fig. 24.

Fig. 25.

Fig. 26.

Fig. 27.

Fig. 28.

Fig. 29.

Fig. 30.   Fig. 31.   Fig. 38.   Fig. 37.

Fig. 32.   Fig. 33.

Fig. 34.   Fig. 35.   Fig. 36.

Fig. 43.   Fig. 42.   Fig. 40.   Fig. 39.

Fig. 41.

◁ 21 Diderot's Encyclopédie, Tome IV, 1764. Items 30-37 show the variations in cut of the thumb pieces and fourchettes for open-fingered gloves; 38 illustrates an ordinary glove of the longer, closer fitting style; 39-42 show the construction of a mitten with a variation in design shown in 43.

22 Mr and Mrs Robert Andrews (detail), by Thomas Gainsborough, 1748. The gloves worn by Robert Andrews are the soft English buff-coloured leather gloves which became a traditional accessory for Englishmen from c. 1740 onwards; the glove held in his right hand has the short vent at the outside edge which was a popular feature of this style.

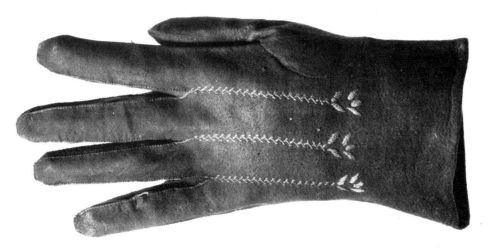

△

24 Man's glove, 1780-1800. Rust-brown suede leather with white silk pointing on the back of the hand; this style of glove was worn also by women for outdoor pursuits, but is mainly associated with men (see fig. 23).

◁ *23 George Drummond, by Thomas Gainsborough, c. 1780. As the century progressed men's gloves became shorter, although natural colours, such as buff, tan and brown were preferred to brighter hues.*

(fig. 24), and many pairs had a slightly curved vent on the outside edge of the gloves (fig. 25).

The dress of these sitters ranged as widely as the dates at which they were painted. There are examples of country, riding, hunting, military and fashionable dress in Gainsborough's portraits, all accompanied by plain, leather gloves. Some pairs have a softer, more supple appearance, but in essence they are all so similar that to date a surviving pair from this period would be immeasurably difficult. The simplicity of style is partly explained by the soft lace or linen ruffles, worn at the wrist, which were an important

25 Trade card of Charles Smith, c. 1750. The glove ▷ *on the trade card is the fashionable men's open vent style (see fig. 22); most glovers' trade cards indicated a wide range of goods, as in this instance, or advertised allied goods such as breeches or perfume.*

CHARLES SMITH,

At the Crown *and* Glove, *near* Bow-Church, CHEAPSIDE, *LONDON*,

SELLS Men's and Women's Bath Lamb-Gloves, and Mittins ; and all other Sorts of Gloves, at Reasonable Rates.

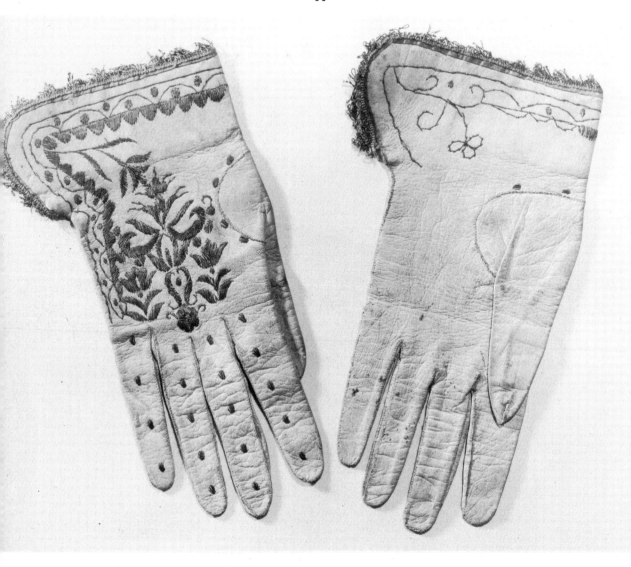

feature of men's dress until the last years of the century, and partly by the concentration of interest on the main items in the male wardrobe at the expense of accessories. All accessories, not just gloves, were understated.

One of the terms most often met with in eighteenth-century descriptions is 'shammy' gloves. Black shammy gloves are often found in connection with the omnipresent mourning gifts. When Dudley Ryder attended his cousin's funeral in 1716 he received 'favours and white gloves', but the principal mourners received black shammy gloves.[6] Fifty-five years later when Parson Woodforde's father was buried, there were black shammy gloves for the pall-bearers and the ladies, the clerk received 'mock shammy' and the

26 Gloves, 1700-1715. Cream kid embroidered with silver thread and trimmed with silver fringed braid; these gloves could have been worn by either sex, and mark the transitional stage between the longer gauntlet gloves of the 1680s and 1690s and the much plainer and shorter open vent gloves worn in town in the 18th century.

under-bearers, sexton and six women wakers (who watched the corpse by night) were given 'black lamb'.[7] Social distinctions of this nature, so assiduously recorded, are a blessing to the costume historian. Shammy gloves, not necessarily black, were

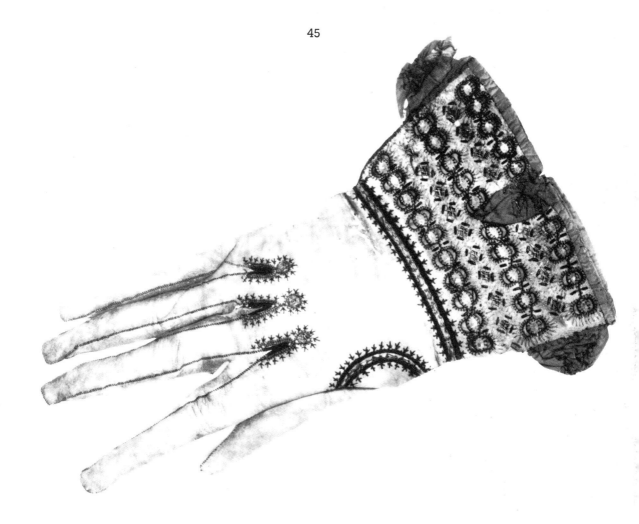

27 One of a pair of women's gloves, 1702. Buff-coloured leather embroidered with plum and black silks and beads, and trimmed with silk rosettes; these gloves are associated with Queen Anne and are highly decorated travelling gloves in the late 17th-century tradition.

made from the skin of the chamois antelope, and oil tanned, but 'mock shammy', a cheaper alternative, were made from sheep or lambskins from which the grain was removed, and then oil tanned to counterfeit genuine chamois.

From about 1770 two other varieties of glove for men are mentioned. The Woodstock gloves, named after the Oxfordshire village where they were produced, were made from the skins of fawns, and were a particularly soft and fine lightweight English leather. York tan gloves were the other popular variety, although on occasion men wore chickenskin or Limerick gloves, imported from Ireland. These were popular with both men and women 'because of their innocent effectual quality of making the hands and arms white, clear, soft and smooth'.[8] The best remembered purveyor of these gloves was Mr Warren who had a perfumer's shop in Coventry Street in London. On one of his shop bills for 1778 he discusses their origins with great delicacy: 'The name induced some to think they were made from the skins of chickens, but on the contrary, they are made of a thin strong leather which is dressed with almonds and spermaceti'.[9] In fact had his customers showed squeamishness at the thought of wearing chicken flesh on their hands, surely they would have been even more disturbed to discover that the skin was that of aborted calves, called morts or slinks in the trade. These gloves were so fine and supple that they were often sold, as a novelty, encased in a walnut shell, and examples of these exist in various public and private collections.

At the beginning of the century women's gloves retained some of the delicate but distinctive embroidery of the last years of the seventeenth century. A pretty pair of cream kid gloves, in the Matthews Collection at Chertsey Museum and dating from around the turn of the century, is embroidered with silver thread in a design of flowers and pomegranates, with a delicate scroll decoration down the outside of the hand and around the wrist, and there are silver dots on the fronts of the fingers and around the thumb. The short gauntlet is edged with short fringed braid, and lined with blue silk (fig. 26). These are probably riding or travelling gloves, but, when compared to the gloves which Queen Anne left at Oxford in 1702, they seem altogether lighter and more eighteenth century in character than those of the queen. The latter, with their elongated fingers and densely embroidered gauntlets with the rosette ribbon trimming seem much more akin to the fashions of the late 1680s and 1690s. They are a reminder of how much fashion is dependent on the tastes of the individual – Queen Anne seemed always more late seventeenth century in her dress than eighteenth century (fig. 27).

As the century progressed women's outdoor gloves became as plain as those worn by men, and it was the indoor longer length gloves and mittens which reflected the prevailing fashions (figs. 20 and 21). The gloves, to judge by surviving examples and the portraits of the century, were disconcertingly plain and of the palest hues, with the exception of mourning gloves, and interestingly, the illustrations in Diderot's *Encyclopédie* show no signs of decoration on the gloves and mittens which were worn by the 1760s. However, in the 1730s there was something of a vogue for gloves with openwork insertions from the palm to the upper edge of the glove. One pair of these, in the collection of the Gallery of English Costume in Manchester, was worn by a bride in 1735. They are white leather edged with a deep band of silver lace with a wide insertion of silver crochet work or 'faggoting' set into the underside of the glove (fig. 28). A similar style exists in the Spence Collection,

---

28 Women's gloves, 1735. White leather edged with silver lace, with an insertion of silver crochet work or 'faggoting' on the underside; these gloves are associated with a wedding of this date.

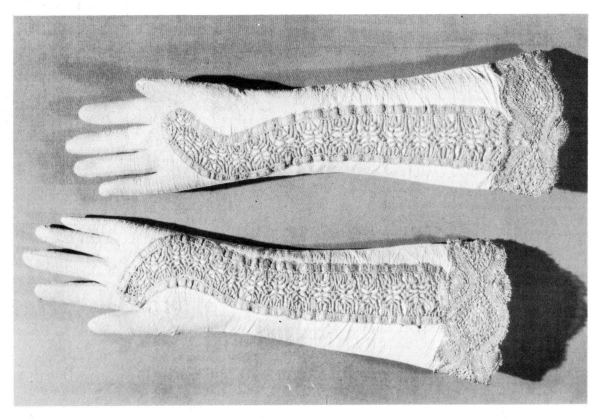

Will Hill Earl of Hillsborough
Margaretta Count[ss] of Hillsborough
Viscount Kilwarlin & Lady Mary Amelia Hill

but in this instance the white glove is edged with a dark green silk braid, and the faggoting is also green. There is a pair of gloves in the collection of Dent Fownes which shows how such a style could be adapted to suit mourning. The gloves are white leather, the insertion is black and there are bands of black silk at the top of the gloves. The effect of gesturing or turning out one's hands, seemingly covered with the plainest leather when in repose, must have been quite dramatic. These pairs of gloves are 'glazed leather', which after the passage of time cracks, marring the good looks of otherwise very fine examples. One reads of 'kid and other gloves gum'd and glaiz'd to great perfection'[10] in the trade cards and bills of the time, but the glazed effect which was so much admired has not lasted well. Similar open-work designs are found on the underside of mittens,

29 1st Marquess of Downshire and his family, by Arthur Devis, c. 1755. Gloves would have marred the effect created by Lord Downshire's gauzy lace sleeve frills, but Lady Downshire and her daughter both wear white, elbow-length mittens; the flaps of Lady Downshire's pair are turned back to reveal a blue silk lining to match her dress.

although the effect is marginally less dramatic as many mittens were made of silk, so that the overall appearance is lighter. Mittens were a popular alternative to gloves throughout the eighteenth century. At the turn of the seventeenth century they were long and narrow; often the curved point which covered the back of the hand was embroidered in richly coloured

30 Woman's mitten, 1750-60. White linen embroidered with red silk; this photograph is a useful illustration of how simple most eighteenth century gloves and mittens were when compared with other fashionable accessories.

silks in a similar fashion to the very late seventeenth-century women's gloves. These peaks are usually lined with plain silk, but later versions reversed this process, leaving the upper side plain, and concentrating the embroidery, or using a fine brocaded silk under the peak, allowing this to be turned back like a decorated cuff (fig. 29).

Many mittens were a plain silk, linen or cotton

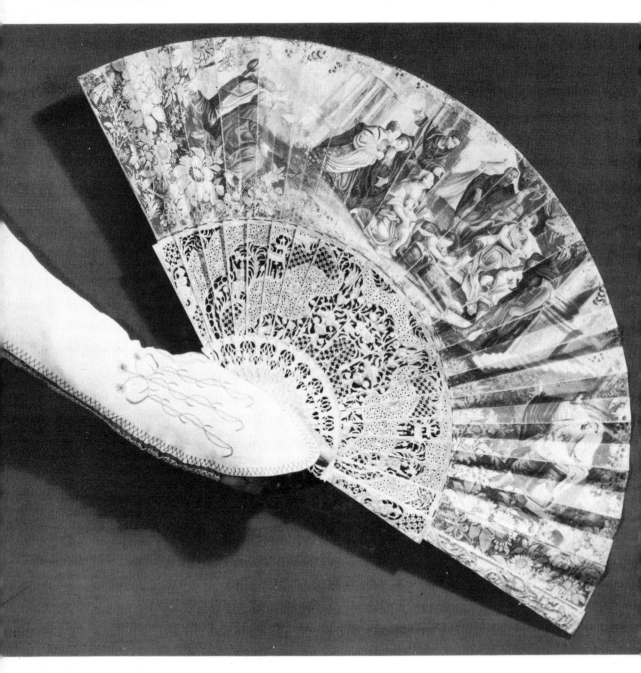

1   Man's glove, 1595-1605. Cream leather and white satin embroidered with polychrome silks, metal threads and spangles, with two bands of pattern, the deeper one incorporating the head of Ceres flanked by cornucopias and phoenixes, the shallower one illustrating various fruits; wrist decoration of ruched silk and metal lace; fringe of silver gilt thread and spangles.

2   Man's glove, 1615-30. Buff coloured leather with a stepped gauntlet of white satin embroidered with metal thread and spangles in a flower and leaf design; trimmed with silver gilt lace; the fingers outlined and elongated by the use of plaited metal braid.

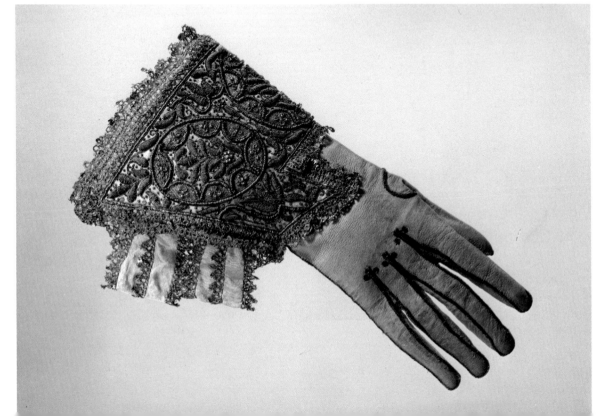

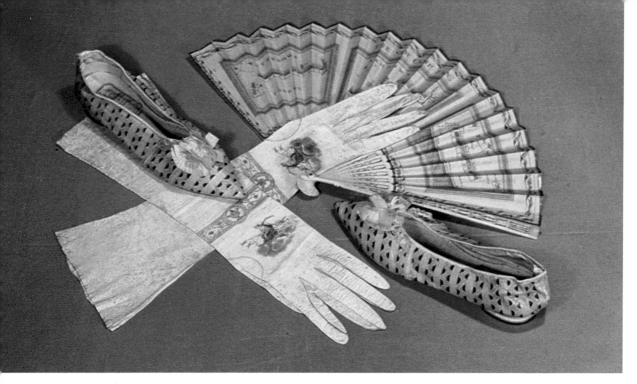

3 Woman's gloves, fan and shoes, 1794-6. The complementary
nature of late 18th century accessories is illustrated by this
group of items; the delicacy of the colours and the finesse
of the printing matched the lighter mood of all women's
clothes at this date; the white kid gloves are printed and
hand coloured.

4 Women's gloves and glove stretchers, 1865-75. Wrist-
length daytime gloves of white kid with scalloped cuffs and
contrast stitching; evening gloves of white kid embroidered
in polychrome silks; the narrowness of the daytime glove
on the left shows the practical need for glove stretchers.

with delicate lines or scrolls of embroidery on the back of the hand and contrast outline stitching around the edges and thumb (fig. 30). The silk mittens, in the weight we should today call taffeta, although in the eighteenth century lustring was the usual name, came in a range of pretty colours, pinks, yellows, blues and greens, and must have been chosen and made to complement the colours of particular dresses. Examples which date from the 1750s and 1760s sometimes have a frill of the same silk at the top of the arm, reflecting the rococo styles of broken decoration and movement on the flat surface of dresses (fig. 31). Other, slightly earlier examples, which date from the 1730s and 1740s are embroidered with strong, decisive bands of flowers and leaves, which reflected the contemporary taste for richly brocaded but naturalistic flowered silks (figs. 31 and 32).

Knitted silk gloves and mittens were also popular, and examples of these are often vibrant in colour with simple, horizontal bands of pattern or complicated vertical designs which include flowers and leaves (fig. 32). Silk gloves and mittens were produced on framework knitting machines in the

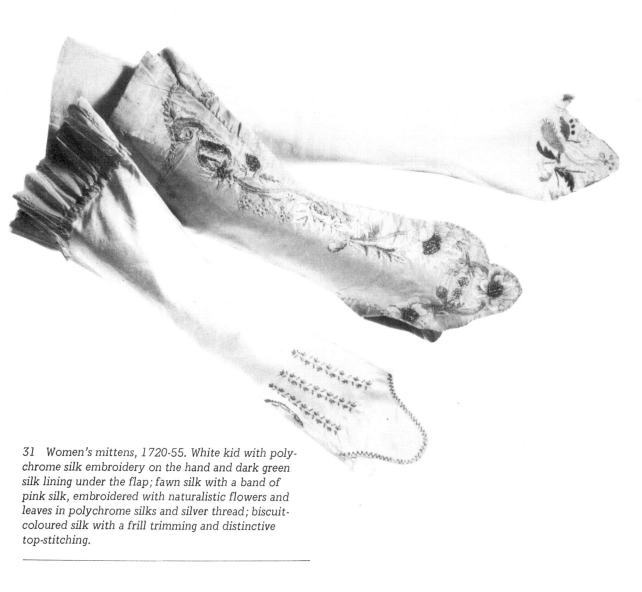

31 Women's mittens, 1720-55. White kid with polychrome silk embroidery on the hand and dark green silk lining under the flap; fawn silk with a band of pink silk, embroidered with naturalistic flowers and leaves in polychrome silks and silver thread; biscuit-coloured silk with a frill trimming and distinctive top-stitching.

32 Women's mittens, 1730-65. This group of leather, silk and knitted silk mittens show the popularity and range of materials used for this type of hand covering; they also demonstrate how, after wear, the fabric varieties became creased and tired; the knitted silk mitten is probably French or Italian.

Midlands, but the surviving examples cannot with any certainty be described as English. The strong colours may indicate foreign imports, but in addition, we know from a petition submitted to Parliament in 1765, that the hosiers, framework knitters and dealers in silk stockings, gloves and mittens in Nottingham and the surrounding district believed that the decay of their industry was attributable to the illegal importation of these types of silk knitted goods from France and Italy.[11]

The novelty or sophistication of foreign goods,

particularly French ones in the case of gloves and mittens, was partly combated by the technical developments in the English industry, which in the last twenty-five years of the century made it possible to produce fancy silk and net mittens which matched the fashionable taste for lighter and softer dress, including accessories. These developments were of greater importance at the beginning of the nineteenth century when the fashion for short-sleeved dresses gave greater scope for invention and novelty of design.

*33 1st Marchioness of Salisbury, by Sir Joshua   ▷
Reynolds, c. 1785. The pale, golden yellow gloves which Lady Salisbury is wearing look so supple and lightweight that they may well be the much admired chickenskin gloves which were reputed to make 'the hands and arms white, clear, soft and smooth.'*

As the century progressed, women's gloves generally became both shorter and plainer. Dresses developed long sleeves, and long, decorated gloves were generally reserved for formal dress occasions. Fortunately there were enough formal events for women's gloves not to become as bland as those worn by the majority of men in the last twenty-five years of the century. In 1774 the *Lady's Magazine* mentions 'Persian gloves, white, and tied on the top of the arm with coloured ribbon'.[12] Glove strings became a feature of long gloves, even to the extent of having 'diamond buckles to the glove strings' at a full dress function in 1783.[13] The problem of all long gloves was their propensity for falling down the arm in unsightly creases, so tying them well above the elbow was a tidy solution. When Mrs Papendiek, as a member of the party which attended George III and Queen Charlotte when they visited the Worcester 'glove manufactory' in 1788, saw the gloves made there, she also mentioned her family's predeliction for 'brown York tan gloves' worn tied high over the elbow, to preserve the arm in beauty for womanhood'[14] (fig. 33).

Although comparatively plain examples of the gloves, in leather or cotton, survive in both public and private collections, the interesting ones, dating from 1790-1800, are printed on a kid leather ground. One pair, which were made by Fownes, the Worcester glove manufacturers, in 1796, are grey with an Adamesque design forming a bracelet around the wrist and thumb, and a pastoral scene of a cottage and tree on the back of the hand. The top of the glove is edged with a narrow band of cream suede which contains the ribbon ties. Another pair, shorter and without ties, survive in the Spence Collection. They are buff-coloured kid, with a 'bracelet' print which includes a neo-classical urn, and the medallion on the back of the hand contains a woman in a mob cap placing a garland of flowers on a lamb. Worthing Museum has a pair in white kid, with a version of the bracelet border, and on the back of the hand there is a goddess in a chariot drawn by birds printed in black, but overpainted with pink, yellow and blue (plate 3).

Although the surviving examples of eighteenth-century gloves are less brilliantly decorated than seventeenth-century ones, many more varieties can be seen and examined, and it is this diversity of materials which is particularly interesting. Diderot's *Encyclopédie* reminds us that glovemaking was still a highly skilled craft, in which leather was the principal material, but many makers and traders of gloves in large cities had diversified to provide other types of merchandize. The trade cards of the eighteenth century, as well as bills and stock inventories, indicate the widening range. One card states, 'Charles Smith, at the Crown and Glove, near Bow-Church, Cheapside, London, sells Men's and Women's Bath Lamb Gloves and Mittins, and all other sorts of Gloves, at Reasonable Rates'.[15] Another card, that of William Stephenson, gives the information that he 'Makes & Sells all Sorts of Kid & other Gloves Gum'd & Glaiz'd to Great Perfection';[16] but in the warehouse behind his shop there was an astonishingly varied stock including clothing, ribbons, jewellery and furs. The two traditional trades with which glovers were associated, perfume distilling and breeches making, continued to be important links. We have already heard of Mr Warren whose chickenskin gloves, discreetly perfumed, formed only one element of his stock in trade. However, it is amusing to find on the trade card of William Pape 'At ye Breeches & Glove' that the major description relates to leather breeches and as an afterthought is added 'NB all sorts of Riding Gloves'[17] (fig. 34).

The fashion for silk, linen and cotton gloves meant that milliners and dressmakers could compete with glovers in supplying these fashionable accessories. Some men specialized in these goods, for instance Thos. Moore, whose trade card in the late 1750s states that he made and sold 'Thread, Cotton, Worsted and Silk Mitts and Gloves'. In country areas or smaller towns the appearance of pedlars, or travelling salesmen from the new manufacturing centres in the Midlands, was an important event. In Samuel Richardson's novel *Pamela*, 'A pair of knitt mittens turned up with white calico' were bought from a pedlar.[18] This was in 1740, but towards the end of the century it was altogether more likely that many items of this sort would be bought in a milliner's shop. When Mrs Elizabeth Brown, a Norwich milliner, was declared bankrupt in 1785, her stock included men's, women's and children's gloves and mittens, as well as fabrics, trimmings, scents, other accessories and the items required for caps, bonnets and hats.[19] The range, and the valuations placed on these gloves and mittens tell us a great deal about the less expensive end of the market, although it should be remembered that gloves, without lavish bullion decoration, were not a great expense. Amongst the recognizable varieties are listed kid, black lamb, worsted, linen and twilled cotton gloves and mittens. The most expensively valued items were men's kid gloves. Although listed as damaged, the eleven pairs were still worth 11 shillings, whilst seventeen pairs of men's white lamb gloves (undamaged) were only valued at 4 shillings 6 pence. Perfect twilled cotton gloves were worth 1 shilling per pair, but thirteen pairs of women's linen

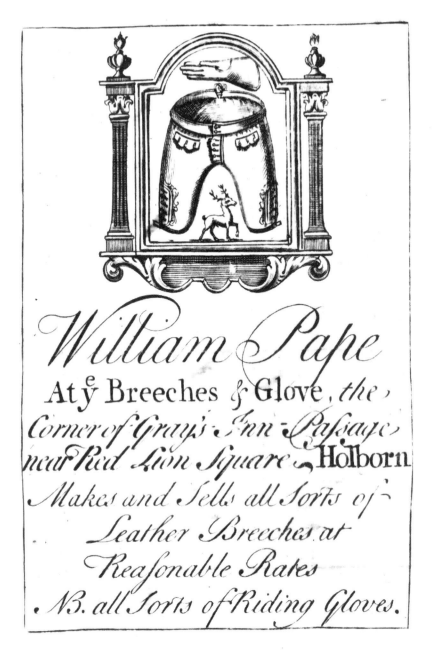

William Pape

At ye Breeches & Glove, the
Corner of Gray's Inn Passage
near Red Lion Square Holborn
Makes and Sells all Sorts of
Leather Breeches at
Reasonable Rates
. N.B. all Sorts of Riding Gloves.

gloves and mittens and six pairs of girls' were valued at just 2 shillings. A pair of black worsted gloves still displayed in the right-hand window of the shop were obviously perfect at 10 pence for the pair, because fifteen damaged pairs were worth only 2 shillings 6 pence.

The fabric and knitted gloves were much cheaper because of the technical revolutions which had placed English textile industries in the van of their competitors by the end of the eighteenth century. Ironically this did not prevent the fashionable world preferring

34 Trade card of William Pape, c. 1758. Many makers of leather riding breeches also provided riding gloves, and they were assured of a good trade in a century when all outdoor and country pursuits became increasingly popular with English gentlemen.

foreign gloves, nor the government from taxing glove-wearers. Smuggling the prohibited foreign gloves into Britain was comparatively easy, as we have already seen from the petition of 1765 concerning French and Italian silk gloves and mittens. Protection for British glovers had been reaffirmed by the government in 1675 and again in 1744,[20] but this did not prevent shrewd British importers and exporters buying French gloves and shipping them, with additional duty on each pair, to the American colonies.[21] The American colonies were a natural export market for English goods, but the War of Independence damaged this trade, and the Leicester knitted glove trade which exported most of its products was adversely affected by the changed circumstances.[22] Although it did not help the knitted sector of the trade, the government, in 1776, produced an Act of Parliament which encouraged the import of kid and lambskins as an aid to the production of good quality goods, and fines on smuggling foreign gloves were more strictly implemented.[23] This Act was aimed particularly at France, the producer of the finest kid gloves, but by the last years of the century various government measures in France, and the inevitable expansion of other countries in the area of glove-making, meant that they were beginning to feel threatened by the Germans, Austrians, Italians and Russians.[24] By the last years of the eighteenth century the number of countries producing stylish and economically attractive gloves was growing, but the results of these changes, although felt by particular areas of the industry, did not cause general concern until some thirty years later.

An additional disadvantage, home grown in this instance, was William Pitt's imposition of stamp duty on gloves in 1785. His estimates of the likely revenue were based on the supposition that approximately three million people bought at least one pair of gloves each year, and that a small, but economically important group bought upwards of twenty pairs. The new tax imposed 1 penny duty on gloves costing between 4 and 10 pence per pair, 2 pence on the 10 pence to 1 shilling 4 pence varieties and 3 pence on gloves costing upwards of 1 shilling 4 pence. The act was not particularly effective and was repealed in 1794, but it can be seen as a warning to the glove trade in Britain that government was not always sure to act in its best interests.

4

Prettiness and Propriety
1800-1899

The early years of the nineteenth century produced a dichotomy in men's and women's fashions which remained unresolved for the following one hundred and twenty years. Men's dress had gradually, in the closing years of the eighteenth century, become more tailored and plain in appearance, but a fashionable line depended upon a smooth and perfect fit which, although elegant in appearance, mitigated against relaxed or careless posture. Women's dress was much softer and more fluid, using light materials and requiring the simplest and most comfortable corsets yet introduced into the female wardrobe, but this happy state of affairs lasted only until the mid-1820s. Slowly but inexorably women's fashions became more rigid and constricting beneath a pretty exterior as men's clothes settled into a sombre, but relatively simple range of coats and trousers which carefully avoided exaggerated or restricted styles. The appearance of a fashionable couple, for most of the century, suggested quiet, businesslike male confidence allied to a pretty, but useless social ornament. Naturally there were exceptions to this rule, but insofar as glove fashions were concerned, we would expect to find continued simplicity in men's gloves, but increased prettiness in women's, and, in essence, that was the state of affairs.

The etiquette of glove wearing was an important feature of nineteenth-century life, and whilst continuing with the traditional seventeenth- and eighteenth-centuries' requirements for mourning gloves, the glove as a wedding favour disappeared. This disappearance is corroborated by one of a set of maxims in an etiquette book published in 1843: 'The custom of sending bridecake and gloves along with the cards of a newly-married couple, has long fallen into disuse. The cards alone are all that are now considered necessary'.[1] However, the occasions on which gloves had to be worn, and the numbers of people who felt they should observe such rules, increased. There was a great deal of social mobility in the nineteenth century as men made their fortunes in industry and commerce, and it was to the members of such families that many

of the flood of etiquette books were directed.

Hints on Etiquette, published in 1837, contains advice for both men and women. If attending a ball, a man was told, 'Do not insist upon pulling off your glove on a very hot day when you shake hands with a lady. If it be off, why, all very well; but it is better to run the risk of being considered ungallant, than to present a clammy ungloved hand.'[2] Both sexes were told that they should 'Always wear your gloves in church or in a theatre',[3] but women were advised 'Ladies should never dine with their gloves on — unless their hands are not fit to be seen.'[4]

The authoritative tone of these maxims brooked no objection; and it is plain that such advice benefited not only the reader but, in passing, glove manufacturers and sellers. Many of the books repeated each other's advice, worded slightly differently, thus strengthening certain traditions whilst scorning others. In 1843 a set of maxims for ladies contained the following advice on the protocol of glove wearing: 'It is not considered proper for ladies to wear gloves during dinner. To appear in public without them — to sit in church or a place of public amusement destitute of these appendages, is decidedly vulgar. Some gentlemen insist on slipping off their gloves before shaking hands; — a piece of barbarity, of which no lady will be guilty.'[5] Ladies also, if they wished to be considered worthy of the name, had to exercise caution over their choice of gloves which ' . . . ought always to harmonise with the rest of the dress. When coloured gloves are worn, the most delicate tints should be chosen. Nothing is so vulgar as an incongruous glaring-coloured glove.'[6]

When gloves were worn they had to be buttoned; for example, in the 1850s, a young girl was rebuked by her mother for wearing her gloves unbuttoned in church: 'But Mamma, what is one to do if one's hands perspire?' 'My love, the perfect lady does not perspire.'[7] The perfect lady was possibly the creation of the etiquette books and the growing number of women's magazines, but this ideal was what many of the newly rich middle classes aspired to be. However, when the highest in the land broke such rules, the arbiters of etiquette had, grudgingly, to accept the change. In 1876 a writer reported, 'The new common habit of girls taking off their gloves in church, although until comparatively lately this would have been considered a terrible breach of propriety; it was,

I believe, Princess Louise who first set at nought this restriction as to remaining gloved through the service.'[8]

Propriety was an important nineteenth-century concept, but today it may seem much more like prudishness. Physical contact, except in the most

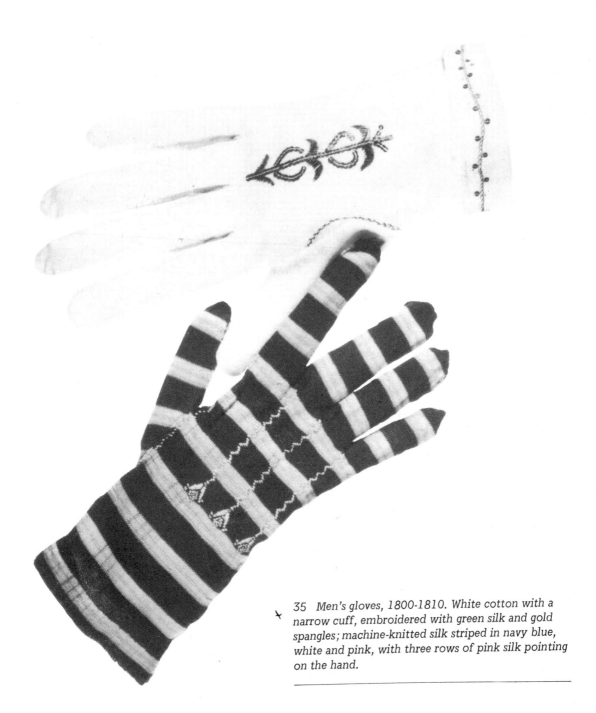

35 Men's gloves, 1800-1810. White cotton with a narrow cuff, embroidered with green silk and gold spangles; machine-knitted silk striped in navy blue, white and pink, with three rows of pink silk pointing on the hand.

private circumstances, was considered distasteful, and when such contact was inevitable, it was usually rendered more acceptable by the interposing of some anonymous material. All servants, for example, had to wear gloves, usually made of some strong white cotton, even when waiting at table, as 'there are few things more disagreeable than the thumb of a clumsy waiter in your plate.'[9]

The gloves which were worn until the mid-1820s were comparatively plain for both sexes. Men's coat sleeves became longer, often well below the wrist, so gloves were single and quite short, although riding gloves were longer and rather fuller around the wrist. Plain leather and cotton gloves were popular and York tan gloves remained fashionable for formal wear. Cotton gloves were invariably white, but sometimes the smallest amount of decoration was applied to the back of the hand, using coloured silk embroidery or sequins (fig. 35). Occasionally one discovers gloves which, in terms of construction, material and length, obviously belong to a particular period, but are of such a startling colour or decoration that they seem atypical. One pair of men's gloves in the Spence Collection, of machine-knitted silk, but cut up and sewn, have horizontal stripes of dark blue alternating with white stripes with a narrow pink band through the centre. They are embroidered with three zig-zag lines of pointing on the back of the hand, and are quite startlingly bright (fig. 35). Possibly there was a brief moment when such brightly coloured gloves were temporarily fashionable, c.1800-1810, because in every other particular they accord with what we know about cut-up silk gloves in that period.

However, generally speaking, the preference was for natural-coloured (buff, tan, yellow) and white kid, doeskin and chickenskin or Limerick gloves, or for white cotton or silk. Worsted gloves were available for the less well-to-do, although according to a contemporary advertisement, leather gloves were not necessarily expensive, being from 10 pence and upwards.[10] Black gloves began to appear as a fashionable accessory for town wear in the 1820s, and not just for mourning, as had previously been the custom. These sombre gloves complemented the discreet dark coats, although an elegant Frenchman, Baron Schwiter, painted by Delacroix in 1826, punctuated his black suit with a brilliantly white stock, grey/white silk socks and buff suede gloves (fig. 37).

Women's gloves were deceptively plain in the early years of the century, although the short white kid gloves printed with either small Jacques Callot figures, swirling lines or diamond patterns, all executed in the highest-quality black printing, perhaps indicate a desire for novelty which was never quite lost sight of amongst the hundreds of plain York tan, Limerick, white and pastel-coloured leathers, silks and nets which followed. These printed gloves, which survive in many collections in England, Europe and the United States of America, were produced in Barcelona around the turn of the century, and provided a virtuoso finale to the vogue for printed gloves which appeared in the last decade of the eighteenth century (fig. 36).

The fashion magazines, which became increasingly influential throughout the century, produced in this period delightful hand-coloured plates showing the latest fashions. These plates were accompanied by descriptive notes, and elsewhere in the magazines were found advertisements placed by the various dressmakers, specialist shops and warehouses which specialized in fashionable items. In *La Belle Assemblée* in 1806, the Nottingham Warehouse at 64 Cheapside advertised 'Long lace mits at 2s. 3d. Long white or coloured silk gloves 3s. 6d. and upwards. A great many . . . women's leather gloves from 10d. and upwards. Also real white kid gloves, very cheap.' Long gloves were worn with the gauzy, short-sleeved dresses, and are illustrated in a kaleidescope of delicate colours in the fashion plates between 1800 and 1825: white, buff, flesh-coloured, yellow, lemon, stone, lilac, blue and pink. In 1807 we are assured that Limerick (chickenskin), York tan and white kid 'are those selected by the female of taste and propriety',[11] and in 1812, after a brief flirtation with buff and coloured gloves for formal evening wear, 'white kid gloves for full dress are once more universal, buff having entirely disappeared.'[12] In such a manner was the less socially confident reader persuaded to conform to the 'proprieties' of the smart world.

If one judges from surviving examples, the more discreet gloves were preferred. Buff suede and yellow chickenskin can be found in some quantity, occasionally leavened by white cotton with a slight trail of embroidery; some silk lace mittens and, more rarely, plain machine-knitted silk gloves. Dent Fownes, in their splendid collection of historic gloves, possess a pair of the last, once worn by the Empress Josephine; they are white, hand-stitched and surprisingly crude in construction. They lack the casual elegance which one finds in fashion plates of the time. However, it should be remembered that fashion plates and to a large extent portraits convey an idealized image, a world of sitters whose clothing is always fresh, clean and uncreased. Gloves with ties at the top of the arm

36 *Women's gloves, c. 1800. White kid printed in black; many pairs of these gloves survive in museum collections; although Spanish in origin, they seem to have successfully evaded the ban on foreign imports.*

continued to be fashionable (fig. 38). There is a portrait by Ingres in the Louvre, of Mademoiselle Rivière, painted in 1805, in which she is wearing buff suede mittens with the white ties dangling free at the outside of the arm.

The social etiquette which required gloves to be worn in almost every possible circumstance should have been of inestimable benefit to the English glove industry, and temporarily this was the case, but in 1825 a change in government policy rocked the industry to its foundations. The prohibition on foreign luxury goods was lifted, and although a small

duty was levied on these goods, the English market was soon flooded by cheap, foreign gloves from Germany, Italy and Austria, and marginally more expensive, but exquisitely made French gloves. As we have seen in earlier chapters, the English admired foreign gloves and there was a small but steady, surreptitious trade in them, but after 1825, they swept all before them. In 1832, exactly 1,516,663 pairs of French gloves were imported legally into England, and the numbers rose throughout the century.[13] When W.H. Hull, a propogandist for the

37 Baron Schwiter, by Eugène Delacroix, 1826. The ▷ unrelieved black of the baron's suit provided a sombre ground against which his plain, buff-coloured leather gloves are distinctive, although in every other way they are unremarkable.

re-establishment of the prohibition or for levying much higher duty, published his book *Gloves and the Glove Trade* in 1834, he charted the collapse of many traditional glovemaking centres. The book makes sad reading and he conveys something of the desperation that must have been felt in the West Country, the Midlands, Yorkshire and Ireland during that period.

By 1838, *The Workwoman's Guide* reported that 'The chief kinds are kid, doe-skin, Berlin, Woodstock and Limerick. The principal manufacturers for the former kinds are at Worcester, Dundee and Jersey; the latter take their names from the places where they are made. French gloves are by some preferred to the English make, as they are considered to be more elastic. The Berlin gloves look like Woodstock, and wash and wear beautifully . . . . Others are made of cotton, silk and worsted, and woven, net or knit.' Berlin leather gloves were not the same as 'white Berlins', which were strong cotton gloves, much worn by household servants. However, from this extract we can judge that the English glove trade in all its areas of operation was adapting itself to changed circumstances. The realization that competing with the fashionable French manufacturers was an uneven battle gradually took hold and, instead, English leather glovemakers concentrated on the plain, rather heavier leather gloves which were ideal for men, for country wear and for sporting activities. Some English manufacturers opened factories in France or reached agreements with leading French companies, who supplied them with fashionable styles, sold by the English firm but containing the French name inside.

In the late 1820s and 1830s, men's gloves underwent a renaissance in the use of colour, with yellow, pink, sky-blue and lilac gloves worn in the daytime in town; doeskin for riding and driving, and white or buff kid for evening wear. Count d'Orsay, the archetypal dandy, on whom the young Disraeli modelled himself, stated unequivocally, 'An English gentleman ought to use six pairs of gloves a day. In the morning to drive a britzska to the hunt, gloves of reindeer. At the hunt, to follow a fox, gloves of shammy leather. To return to London in a Tilbury, after a drive at Richmond in the morning, gloves of beaver. To go later for a walk in Hyde Park, or to conduct a lady to pay her visits, coloured kid gloves, braided. To go to a dinner party, yellow dog's-skin gloves. And in the evening, for a ball or rout, gloves of lamb-skin, embroidered with silk.'[14] It is doubtful whether the majority of men, fashionable or otherwise, were inclined to follow Count d'Orsay's advice. The cost of the gloves alone would have made such fastidiousness

prohibitive, but this description gives us useful information on the range which was available. The construction and fit of the gloves improved in the 1840s and 1850s, due partly to the increased publicity and manufacturer's interest given to Xavier Jouvin's new system of glove calibres (see Chapter 1), reversing the statement, given in *The Workwoman's Guide* of 1838, that 'It is impossible to give any shapes or scales for gloves; the best plan to get an exact pattern is to pick an old glove to pieces, and cut by it.' A well-fitting glove was an important complement to the tailored appearance of men's clothing, particularly when the glove was plain, usually decorated only with three rows of stitching or pointing on the back of the hand. A better fit was also ensured by buttoning the glove at the back of the wrist so that it fitted smoothly, and after about 1855 when M. Raymond of Grenoble introduced the dome or snap fastener, these gradually started to appear, and are an aid to dating gloves of uncertain mid-nineteenth century provenance.[15]

The attributes of the perfect lady, the ideal to which many nineteenth-century writers and journalists in women's magazines directed the aspirations of the susceptible, included small hands and small feet. Hands could be made to appear smaller by being mercilessly crammed into tight gloves (it is no accident that glove stretchers appeared at this time to assist the vain purchaser in easing their gloves), or by choosing gloves or mittens which are so decorated that the hand appears smaller both in length and width.

Women's day dresses from the mid-1820s onwards were long-sleeved, and the line of the sleeve never crept higher than the elbow throughout the century, although evening dresses were often both alarmingly decolleté and excessively short-sleeved. Evening gloves and mittens came just below the elbow until about 1840 when they decreased quickly to wrist length, remaining at that line until the mid-1860s. Day gloves, and mittens, equally popular in the 1830s and 1840s, were wrist length or slightly longer (figs. 39 and 40). The decoration on both day and evening gloves, and the fashionable materials, were similar: light-coloured leather (usually kid) 'which can only be worn for one day',[16] knitted gloves, silk net in pastel shades, white, and in the case of net mittens,

---

38 Fashion plate, 1818. For Court dress or formal ▷
evening dress gloves tied 'high above the elbow'
continued to be worn into the 1820s both in France,
as illustrated in this plate, and in England.

x

39 *Women's gloves, 1825-40. White kid embroidered with flower and leaf designs using gold or silver thread or polychrome silks; this style of embroidered glove, with small variations in design and length, was popular for nearly twenty years.*

black (fig. 41). Silk or metal thread embroidery of flowers either formed a concentrated design on the back of the hand or were scattered in springs over the whole back of the glove (fig. 42). Evening gloves often had scalloped edges if made of leather; or ribbon, fringe or ruching if made of silk net.

After 1842 another source of information becomes available for dating items of clothing, namely the patent registration files. To work through all of these, and then to trace the success or failure, in terms of the response of the buying public, to these patented designs, would take several years of research, but it is interesting to introduce a random selection, either because they accurately reflect what was popular, or because they demonstrate the Victorian genius for absurdity or innovation for its own sake.[17]

These registrations contain actual samples and drawings or, rather later, photographs of the item in question. In 1843-4 two manufacturers registered designs which would make women's gloves fit better. Charles Topham and Edmund Alderson Fawcett of

Derby patented a glove with india rubber strands knitted into the fabric, whilst Joseph Weldin of Worcester registered a design for an elasticated wrist.[18] Three years later in 1846, William Goddard of Leicester sent a lilac knitted-silk glove with an elastic wrist to be registered.[19] Worthing Museum has mittens, one white and one black with bead and 'gemstone' decoration on the back of the hand, both of which are elasticated at the wrist, and fit stylistically into this early to mid-1840s period when elastication (which in an embryonic form appeared in 1835) was a cause for competition between manufacturers.

By the 1850s the majority of men had eschewed

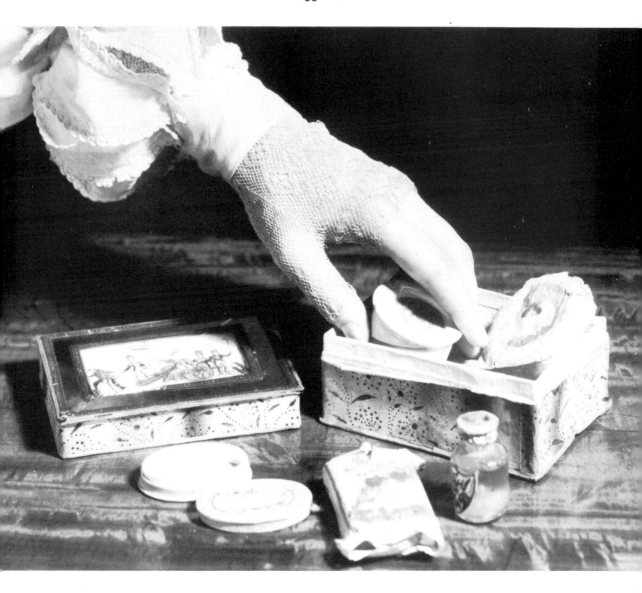

brightly coloured gloves, tending to prefer brown, navy, dark green or black leather in town with contrasting or complementing silk embroidered points (fig. 43). White was *de rigueur* for formal evening wear and stout buff or tan leather was worn in the country. The vulgarity of coloured gloves was left to 'city clerks, dashing young parties who purchase pea-green, orange and rose-pink gloves' at the end of the decade,[20] although lavender gloves were to be seen on the bridegroom at smart weddings (fig. 44).

In 1860 the small remaining import duties on foreign luxury goods were repealed, but without the drastic consequences of the 1825 action. English manufacturers had concentrated their energies on

40   Woman's mitten, 1825-30. White netted silk; light, open-weave mittens were a pretty and comfortable fashion for keeping the hands covered in a period of increasing prudery.

particular styles and weights of glove, and were already well on their way to cornering the market in men's gloves and heavier grade gloves generally. This was probably due in part to the skill of the manufacturers, but also to the knock-on effect of the widespread European admiration for English men's clothing. English menswear was the mark of the inter-

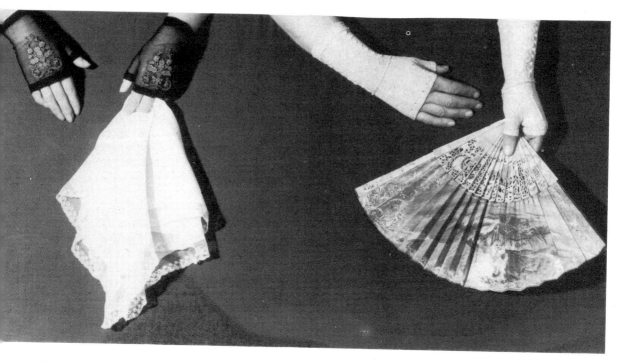

national gentleman in an age when France led the field in all women's fashions.

There comes a point when fashions become so traditional, so understated that little can usefully be said about them. This is true of men's gloves in the last thirty or forty years of the nineteenth century. They were worn everywhere, they came in various subdued shades, fawn kid or grey suede with frock or morning coats, or at weddings, tan with lounge suits, and plain white or cream suede stitched with black for evening wear. Manufacturers tried ingeniously to introduce novelties which would extend the range; in 1877 eyelet hook fastenings were introduced,[21] in 1896 Fownes introduced a patent button on which the smoker could strike his match, and the following year they recommended with the slogan, 'Reins Cannot Slip Rain or Shine', a cape-leather, wide-cut gauntlet glove with ribbed fingers for driving. No consumers can ever have had such a wide range of clothing to choose from as those of the late nineteenth century.

It was also possible to economize by making gloves,

42 *Women's mittens, 1840-45. Cream cotton and black silk net embroidered in a flower design with beads, gold and silver thread and green and red silk; black net mittens were worn a good deal with semi-formal evening dress.*

and in addition to extolling the virtues or lack of vulgarity of certain styles or social practices as opposed to others, the more down-market women's magazines produced notes on netting, knitting, crocheting or otherwise constructing small accessories like home-made gloves and mittens. One surviving pair, probably dating from the late 1840s or 1850s, is of knitted white cotton covered in bands of coloured beads knitted rather in the form of a sampler to show the widest ranges of patterns and colours which could be incorporated. A red cord is threaded around the wrist, and the hapless owner's initial E is forever recorded on the back of the hand (fig. 45). The supplement to the *Lady's Newspaper* in 1856 provides a pattern for knitted 'Gauntlet Mittens' of Berlin wool threaded with sarsnet ribbon, which were intended to be worn over gloves. 'For extra warmth or to protect the glove?' one is tempted to wonder. In 1890 the *Young Ladies' Journal* gave a pattern in one size only which produced a glove suitable for a woman with large hands or a man with small hands,

◁ 41 *Photograph of three girls, by Octavius Hill, 1845-50. The taller of the three girls is wearing wrist-length black net mittens with a semi-formal evening dress; mittens were a perfectly acceptable alternative to evening gloves when worn by the very young or the very old.*

◁ 43 *Prince Albert, photograph 1854. The simplicity of the prince's gloves is in keeping with the sober and businesslike appearance of the rest of his dress.*

↳

44 *Gloves, 1860-80. Short leather gloves with long lines of pointing on the back of the hand were worn by men and women of all classes in the latter half of the 19th century; their superb fit and subtle colours made them elegant accessories.*

although whether either sex would have appreciated this curious sizing is doubtful. However, the gloves, knitted on four No. 16 pins, took 1¾ ounces of Andalusian wool, and can be viewed as the archetypal fore-runners of all the twentieth-century knitting patterns which adapted a simple ribbed glove to fit men, women and children.

Buttoned gloves are a nineteenth-century commonplace, and button size often confuses the unwary. It is only really applicable to women's gloves, and initially can be taken quite literally; eight button gloves did have exactly that number of buttons in the 1870s, but as gloves became longer and longer and buttoning such a time-consuming task, a new type of glove was introduced, the 'Mousquetaire' which, whatever its length, was only buttoned just inside the wrist with four to six buttons. After this innovation,

one reads of 'button-length', which is the meansurement, in inches, from the base of the thumb to the top of the glove.[22]

Generally speaking, women's daytime gloves remained short until the early 1860s, when gauntlet gloves entered the fashionable scene for limited use with yachting jackets. These gloves came in a wide range of colours even when quite plain; in 1854, 'Garnet, pensée, Napoleon, groseille, olive, Adelaide, Rubis, Mazzogram, maroon, myrtle, Tracarad, coffee, Cuba' were advertised, but they also often sported decoration of one sort or another. In 1851, the year of the Great Exhibition, George Shore of 488 New Oxford Street and Deptford in London, patented two appropriate souvenir gloves. The first was of white kid with the Crystal Palace printed on the back, the second was printed with a map of London, reserving the Crystal Palace for the palm.[23] Not at all the style for the lady of propriety and taste! However, there were other, more acceptable novelties available, gloves with ribbons threaded through the wrist in the 1850s, with flower points, with swansdown trimming the wrist, or silk fringing which picked up the flowers embroidered on the hand and, in the 1860s, gloves with a back opening of eyelet holes through which

45 *Woman's glove, 1850-60. Hand-knitted white* ╳ *cotton interspersed with brightly coloured beads, with a narrow red cord threaded through the wrist; patterns for this type of domestic knitting were published in women's magazines of the time.*

silk cords terminating in tassels were threaded. The last were patented in 1866; the examples registered were of fawn suede with red and silk points on the hand and red silk cord and tassels.[24] A pair of this type can be found in the collection of the Gallery of English Costume, Manchester, but are of white kid with brown points and a cream cord and tassels (fig. 46). The registered entries for the same year also described a pair of black kid gloves with a white insertion.[25] A more exotic version of these can be found in the Dent Fownes collection, of blue leather, with a white leather wrist band, tan leather cuff and two blue fingers, one white finger and thumb and a tan finger. This pair is French, marked with the stamp

of Fontaine Fils, the distinguished French manufacturers with whom Fownes traded in the nineteenth century.

Evening gloves became longer in the mid-1860s, and by 1871, 'with the open sleeve, long kid gloves with 8 to 10 buttons have come in again.'[26] The length increased to fifteen buttons by the late 1870s; the patent registers included examples of exquisitely embroidered kid gloves which mirrored the French taste for decorated semi-formal and formal gloves[27] (plate 4). When Princess Louise of Prussia married the Duke of Connaught in 1879 she wore white kid gloves embroidered with a bracelet design of flowers around the upper arm and a matching spray on the back of the hand. These gloves survive in the Museum of London's collection, and can be associated, stylistically, with many pairs in the Dent Fownes collection, and with the whole kidskin, embroidered with multi-coloured silks and metal thread showing a wide range of decorative points, flower sprays, monograms, coronets which is labelled 'Gloves Made to

46 Woman's gloves, c. 1866. White kid stitched with brown silk and laced with a cream silk cord; women's daytime gloves were rarely as plain as men's gloves, and often sported small, fashionable features such as this lacing.

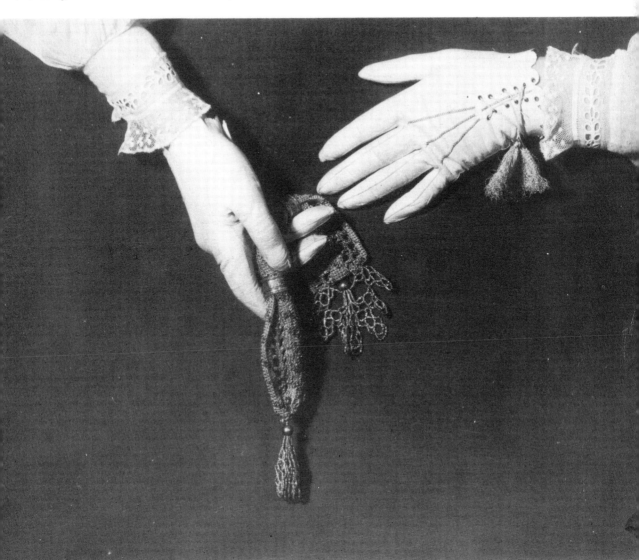

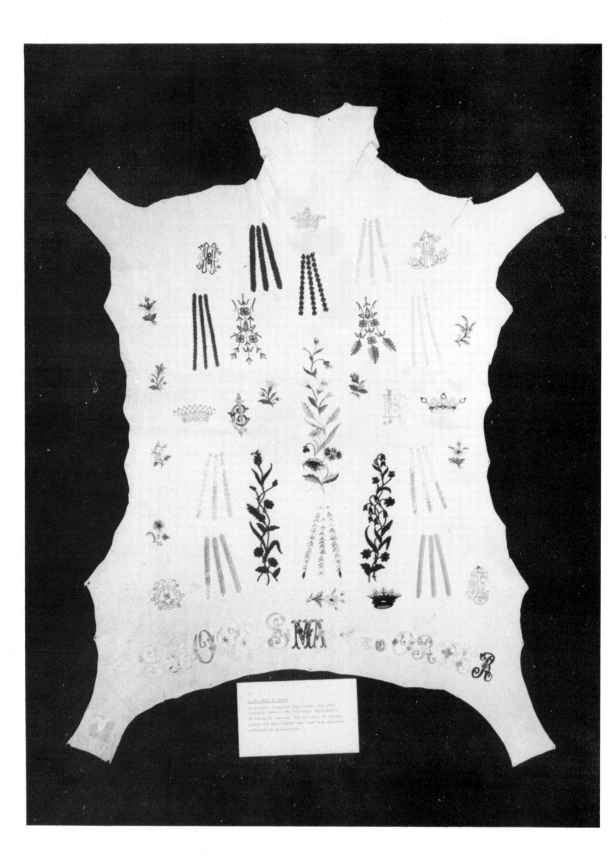

Order', and was a sample for specialist glove shops of the time (fig. 47).

In the last quarter of the century all women's clothing was highly decorated, with the surface of dresses broken up with ruching, frills, fringes, lace and embroidery. Small accessories like gloves, hats, fans and shoes were jerked out of the functional sphere by the use of printing, embroidery, beads and lace (plate 5). The length of both fashionable daytime and evening gloves increased, allowing plenty of scope for inventive decoration (fig. 48), and suede came back into fashion alongside the smooth, classic kid gloves.

However, suede was obviously considered too new-fangled, because in 1882 it was reported, 'Her Majesty has forbidden suede gloves to be worn in the Drawing rooms; these are therefore no longer admissable in dress circles'.[28] The etiquette attached to gloves continued to be debated with great seriousness in both women's magazines and etiquette books. Some amusing expedients were adopted as gloves became longer and tighter, and in *Manners and Social Usages*, published in 1884, the author noted 'Formerly brides removed the whole glove; now they adroitly cut the finger of the left hand glove so that they can remove

◁ *47 White kidskin, 1870-90. This whole skin, embroidered with polychrome silks and gold thread, displays some of the wide range of decorative embroidery which could be worked on custom-made gloves.*

48 Women's glove and mitten, 1875-85. White kid glove embroidered with red, green and gold silks; American mitten with grey knitted silk lower arm, knitted lace upper arm and trimming of grey lace and taupe ribbon.

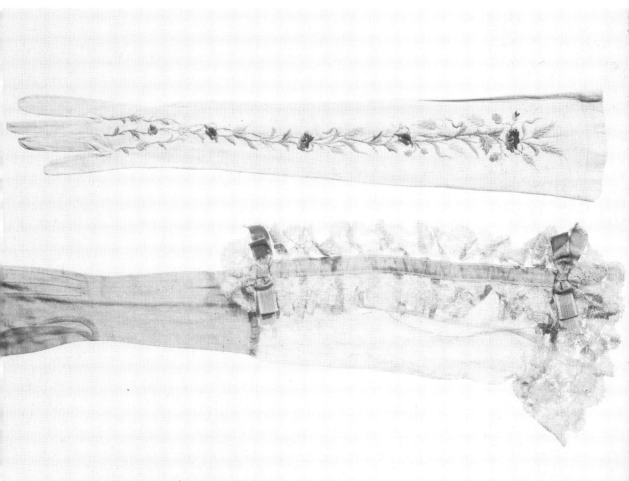

49 *Advertisement from* Le Moniteur de la Mode, *1885. The gloves worn by the model have leather* hands and lace effect arms; *this combination was popular in the 1880s and 1890s for both day and evening wear.*

5 Women's gloves, 1880-90. Beaded gloves were fashionable in the 1880s, and ranged from discreetly decorated examples like the white kid ones, to the most exuberantly brilliant, represented here by bronze leather and net.

6 Women's gloves, c. 1897. White kid gloves embroidered as souvenirs of Queen Victoria's diamond jubilee in 1897; the cream leather gloves with the red, white and blue may have been intended for less flamboyant patriots.

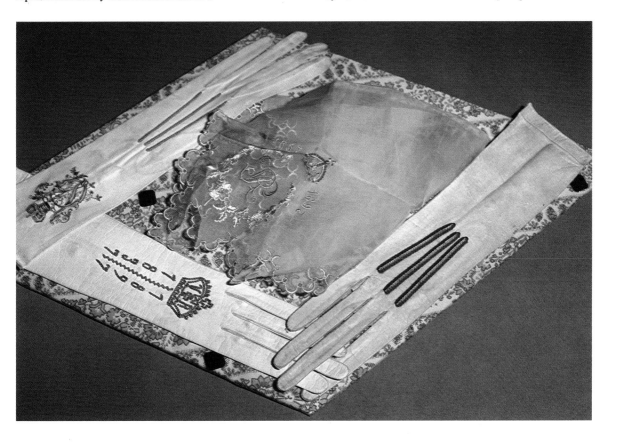

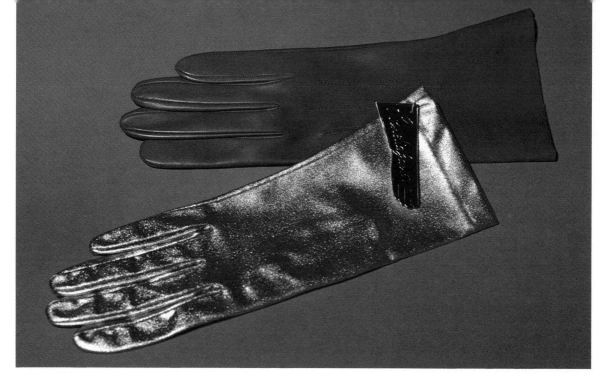

7 Women's gloves, 1978-9. Purple kid gloves made for the spring range of Kir Gloves in 1979; gold lurex gloves made for the winter range by Cornelia James 1978-9; these gloves are the classic late 20th century length and style, and rely for their impact on excellent cut and fit and dramatic colours.

8 Women's gloves, c.1975. Calico gloves, screen printed in the Fauvist manner by Lesley Sunderland; these belong to a series of gloves based on the artist's observation of her own hand, but were never marketed.

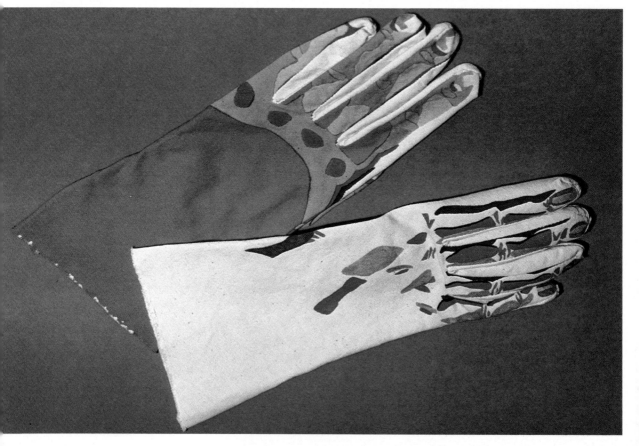

50 Woman's glove, c. 1885. Light brown kid hand,
netted silk arm with appliqué decoration; the similarity
between this surviving example and the gloves in
fig. 49 is very close.

THE LONDON GLOVE COMPANY'S
❖ GLOVES. ❖

"Cinderella" Suède, 12-Button Mousquetaire, 2/6 per pair; 16-Button ditto, 3/3 per pair; 20-Button ditto, 3/11 per pair. In White, Cream, Pink, Lavender, Biscuit, and Tan Shades.

Pure Silk, Perfect Fitting, 12-Button Length Jersey, 1/9 per pair; 16-Button ditto, 1/11 per pair; 20-Button ditto, 2/4 per pair. In Black, White, and all Colours.

Kid Gloves, 4-Button, 2/2 per pair; 6-Button, 2/9 per pair; 8-Button, 3/3 per pair; 12-Button or Mousquetaire, 3/11 per pair. In Black, White, Tans, and Light Shades.

A Detailed Price List, Illustrated, of all Makes will be forwarded Post Free upon Application.

Superior Quality French Kid, 4 Buttons, 2/6 per pair; 6 Buttons, 3/3 per pair. In Black, White, and all Colours.

Heavy Chevrette, English Make, 4 Buttons, 3/3 per pair. In Black, Tans, and Dark Colours.

Driving, Heavy Tan Cape, with Double Spear Points, 3/6 per pair.

Cashmere, 4-Button Length Jersey, 9d. per pair; 6-Button ditto, 10d. per pair; 8-Button ditto, 1/- per pair. In Black and all Colours.

Gentlemen's Dress Gloves, from 5/9 per half doz.; 1/- per pair.

Ladies', Gentlemen's, and Children's Lined and Woollen Gloves of every description.

Postal or Post Office Orders to be made payable to S. A. WORSKETT at the G P.O.

THE LONDON GLOVE COMPANY,
45A, CHEAPSIDE, E.C.

that without pulling off the whole glove for the ring.'[29] The tightness of gloves was essentially due to female vanity, and it had been noted in 1882 that '. . . there are numerous complaints of their bursting owing to their being worn so tight. A few years ago sizes were 6½ to 8½; the majority sold being 7¼ to 7½; now these are 5½ to 6¾.'[30]

Mittens had remained a favourite with older women, but they also re-entered the fashionable wardrobe in the late 1870s. The writer of a column in *The Ladies' Gazette of Fashion*, who described herself as 'Une Parisienne', commented that 'Fastening eight and even sixteen buttons is too intolerable a bore for hot weather, and indolence has prompted many fair excursionists to provide themselves with a good stock of mittens. But, reader mine, beware of the treacherous little mittens: if they enhance the beauty of aristocratic hands, they reveal as glaringly the defects of others, and besides, to be truly elegant, form rather expensive items; those in Chantilly costing about £4, and those in Venetian guipure from £2 to £3'[31] (fig. 48). As always, many manufacturers produced cheaper alternatives, and in the 1880s and 1890s gloves and, more rarely, mittens were produced which had a leather or fabric hand with a silk mesh or net arm, the latter embroidered or covered with appliqué work to simulate lace (figs. 49 and 50). Dent Fownes have various pairs of these, ranging from dramatic black, to ecru with bronze bead embroidery, to white with fine net arms appliquéd with satin butterflies. The ingenuity and range of decoration is delightful, although possibly the most aesthetically pleasing are the gloves which are white suede but printed above the wrist in black to simulate exactly black Chantilly lace. By 1897 it was possible to buy kid evening gloves with lace arms for as little as 6 shillings 10 pence per pair, a far cry from £2 to £4 paid for the exquisite mittens of 1879.

Daytime gloves were made in all colours, although by the end of the century, pearl grey, pale tan and white were emerging as 'classic' favourites. Gauntlets which had appeared in the 1860s continued to be worn for sporting functions, and by the 1890s were considered suitable for garden parties, and other semi-formal outdoor activities. The range of gloves, which increased throughout the century, reflected both the growing number of shoppers and their constant search, by women, for novelties (plate 6), and the more sophisticated shops which catered to their needs (fig. 51). A review of retailing in England during the first half of the century provides information on the growing number of retail and wholesale glovers in major cities. In Manchester in 1822 there were 27 retail hosiers and glovers, but no wholesale glovers; by 1834 there were 33 retail outlets and five wholesale houses, and by 1851 the numbers had risen to 87 and eight respectively.[32] Gloves were sold in the fancy goods sections of drapers' shops and with the emergence of departmental shops in the 1860s, gloves were given a section of their own in these new consumer palaces. Specialist shops continued to attract custom, and the traditional association between glovers and perfumers was continued by Rimmel at their shop in The Strand, London which sold only perfumed gloves, and by L.T. Piver, Perfumer and Glover, who stocked the finest quality French gloves in his London and Paris shops.[33] At the turn of the century gloves seemed an indispensable accessory, although in 1898 one magazine noticed that 'It is rare to see gloves worn except out walking, while in the country many ladies never wear gloves at all.'[34]

◁ 51 *Advertisement from* Sylvia's Home Journal, *1890. Apart from providing a good deal of information about the range and cost of gloves, this advertisement also indicates the fashion for excessively long evening gloves, worn ruched below the elbow.*

5

The Growth of Informality
1900-1980

It is difficult, with hindsight, not to view the twentieth century so far as a period of decline in the history of gloves and glovemaking. The gradual falling off in glove wearing was being noticed as early as 1921 by Eldred Ellis when he recorded 'so far as dress gloves are concerned, . . . a few years ago no gentleman would appear at a dinner or dance without a pair; to-day they are rarely used except at Court or state functions.'[1]

Two world wars and the consequent social, industrial and economic changes have transformed a world, which in 1914, although troubled by changing social standards, seemed likely to recover its former equilibrium once the war was over by Christmas, as many thought likely. The pre-war period, usually thought of as Edwardian, although Edward VII died in 1910, has acquired a nostalgic glamour as the last great age of confidence in established standards of social behaviour (fig. 52). Many of these standards were being questioned or challenged: by women actively demanding the vote, by vibrant and barbaric artistic innovations in painting, ballet, opera and the threatre, and not least by a new attitude towards women's clothing, pioneered by the French designer, Paul Poiret. Individuality was gradually asserting itself over propriety.

Ironically, the technical developments taking place in the preparation of leather for glovemaking from the late nineteenth century onwards were also increasing the flexibility of choice, and making it possible to spend less money on the finished product. These same developments were also slowly undermining, in the long term, an industry which had reached enormous heights of technical and decorative skill by 1900. In Chapter 2, the detailed changes in fabric glovemaking which made inexpensive alternatives to leather gloves more acceptable, were outlined. The major advantage of fabric gloves was that they were washable as well as comparatively inexpensive.

Attempts to find a leather which was comparable in finish and appearance to the highly regarded French kid was spear-headed by the glovemakers in Saxony, Austria, Luxembourg and Belgium whose efforts to up-grade the appearance and feel of lamb-skins were assisted by the introduction of chrome tannage in 1885. This type of mineral tannage produced leather which was water-resistant, hard-wearing and attractive to look at and to wear. During the period leading up to the 1914-18 war, many European countries or states, including those already mentioned, and, in addition, Belgium, Bavaria, Italy and Denmark, were producing a wider range of cheap leather gloves, using nappa, imitation mocha and wash leather. The last name is deceptive, and was, in reality, our old friend 'shammy leather', but now simulated in sheep or lambskin rather than made of the more expensive chamois. All manufacturers perceived the advantage in being able to produce genuinely washable gloves, and between 1913 and 1918 the American leather dressers, using and adapting the mineral tannage process on skins from the Cape and Port Elizabeth districts of South Africa, succeeded in producing washable cape gloves.[2]

Although the correctness of wearing certain types of glove with particular clothes in specific circumstances was important in the early years of this century, the rigid etiquette of the nineteenth century gradually disappeared. Men's gloves continued to be plain and inconspicuous, but it was essential to have a 'wardrobe' of gloves, much in the manner of Count d'Orsay in 1820s and 1830s, in order to be correctly attired for every occasion. There were temporary fads for certain materials and colours, for instance Eldred Ellis noted that, 'A few winters before the war a sudden craze set in for white woollen gloves. Half the men in the country seemed

52 Fashion illustration from The Queen, *1900.* ▷
Formal evening dress in the early years of the 20th century was always accompanied by 20 button kid gloves, although these were usually of the Mousquetaire variety.

to be wearing them, and the glove trade had much to do to meet the demand.'[3] Such crazes were, and are, a nightmare for manufacturers of fashionable goods, for as soon as they were able to adjust their production levels satisfactorily the fashion had already passed, and they were left with an unwanted glut of the item.

However, apart from such temporary distractions, the men's gloves in the pre-1914 period conformed to certain agreed colours, weights and styles which suited the time of day and place. In town the fashionable man wore tan, buff, grey or black cape leather, kid or doeskin gloves, with three rows of pointing on the back, fastened by one or two buttons or dome snap fasteners. At evening functions kid, suede and fabric gloves of white, beige or grey were worn. Gauntlet gloves were worn for driving, and in the winter, lined gloves, with wool or fur linings, were favoured.

Men's clothes retained the sober, serious-minded appearance which had developed in the nineteenth century, and the plainest type of accessories were the most suitable. Women's dress, however, gradually loosened up in the pre-war period. It became rather less constricting, although it lost none of its femininely decorative quality, but gloves became plainer, as if they were unintentional harbingers of future fashions (fig. 53). Daytime colours for suede or leather gloves echoed men's, with the emphasis on tan, brown, black, grey, white and lavendar. The fashionable length varied between four and six buttons. Gauntlets were worn for riding or driving, and in the evening pastel shades appeared, on twelve to sixteen button length suede, kid or silk gloves. It was still possible to buy a wide variety of additional colours and styles, executed in the wide range of leathers, fabrics and wools; the fierce competition between the increasing number of glovemaking nations ensured extensive choice in both quality, design and price.

Today we are accustomed to viewing the First World War as a horrific and cataclysmic event, and those who lived through it suffered hardship and personal tragedies on a scale which have not been equalled since. Much of this was due to the lack of preparation for such a lengthy and, ultimately, worldwide conflict. Ironically, the type of luxuries which were unobtainable in Britain during the Second World War could still be acquired; in 1917, for example, Lady Cynthia Asquith recorded in her diary a gift of gloves from a friend, 'I expected two pairs of gloves, the book [her present to him] having cost 7s.6d. What was my amazement, when I opened the boxes he had bought, to find one dozen white washing gloves, one dozen beautiful suede ones, and a handsome fur-lined pair thrown in, too!'[4] Rather further down the social scale, *Weldons Practical Knitter* was advising its readers to make 'Canadian Gloves . . . of a thumb and a bag for the fingers. They will be found very comfortable to draw over the hands when walking in the garden on a windy day and also for wearing over kid gloves in very cold weather or when travelling.'[5]

The diminishing availability of leather for glovemaking, and the lack of normal trade between Britain and continental European countries inevitably led to a reduction in the supply of gloves. Leather was needed for military uses, including the manufacture of heavy sheepskin gloves with the wool inside, for soldiers serving in the trenches and in motor transport divisions. The majority of troops relied on knitted 'home comforts', including gloves and mittens, because the widespread food shortage led to the slaughter of many animals who were normally reserved for gloving leather.[6] By 1919, shortly after the war ended, the supplies of leather which were available for glove manufacturers had dropped by almost 75 per cent from normal pre-war standards, and all leather was fiercely competed for by other industries. The price of leather dressing materials, and the cost of wages had also risen alarmingly.[7] French suede gloves which had cost 2 shillings 11 pence per pair in 1912, had risen to 8 shillings 6 pence in 1919 (fig. 54).

In the 1920s and 1930s the male attitude towards gloves had, in an embryonic form, reached that which the majority of people hold today. In essence gloves were regarded as practical, functional items which afforded protection from the elements or acted as a buffer, or occasionally might be required with formal dress (fig. 55). The magazines and catalogues of the inter-war period indicate the preferences of the male population. By 1929 it was possible to buy chamois, reindeer, pigskin and antelope gloves 'in every colour' from 8 shillings 6 pence upwards, white evening gloves for 6 shillings 6 pence and 'bleached leather' yachting gloves at 10 shillings 6 pence per pair from H.J. Nicoll & Co. Ltd in Regent Street, London. Sporting gloves were much favoured by manufacturers and customers alike, in 1934 Jaeger were selling woollen skating gloves at 4 shillings 6 pence a pair (fig. 56); by 1937 Harrods were advertising 'chamois-coloured sheepskin' golf gloves with ventilated palms and four round openings across the knuckles to assist total flexibility of the hand. Simpsons sold two varieties of hacking glove, hand-knitted string for town wear, and string-backed and

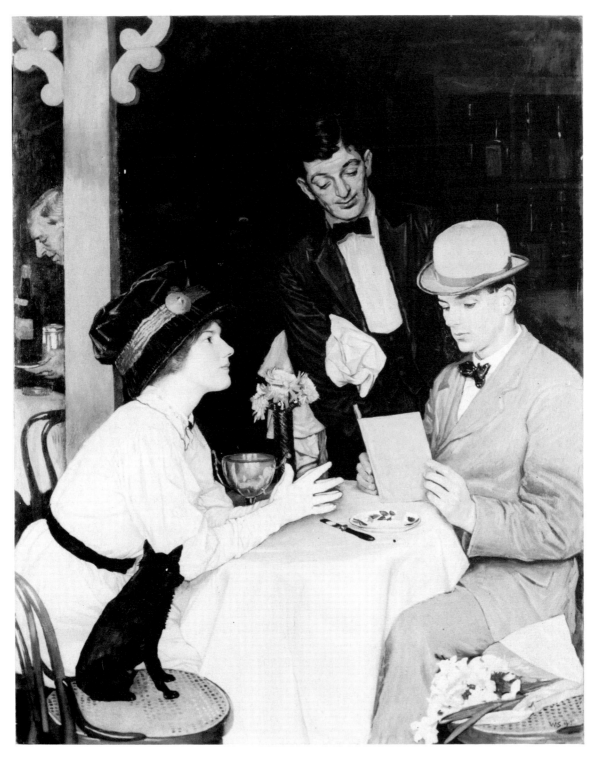

53 'Bank Holiday', by William Strang, 1912. Despite the increasing informality of female dress, young women usually kept their gloves on in public places, although there are no signs that the young man in this picture owned a pair of gloves.

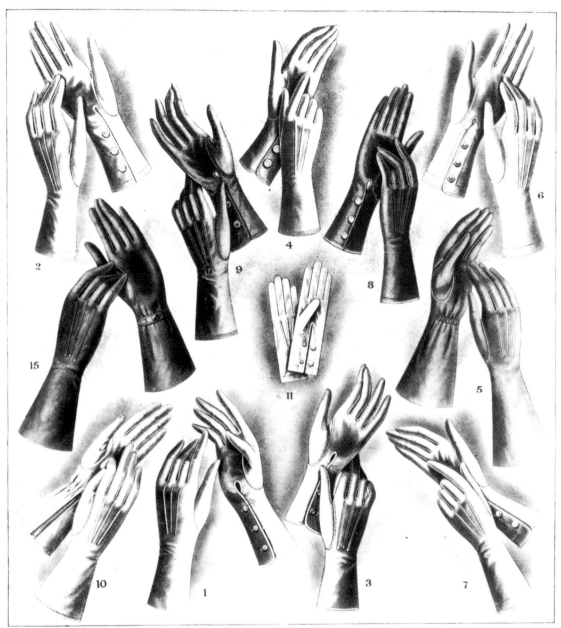

L.G. 1. French Suede. Best quality, white, grey, beaver, mole, lace, pearl, and black   **8 6**

L.G. 2. French Kid. Excellent in wear, 3-button. Beaver, drab, mole, black, and white   **8 11**

L.G. 3. Washable Doeskin. 2-button. White only **7 11**

L.G. 4. Washing Gloves. Good quality doeskin, in white and chamois, hand-sewn black, 2-button   **9 11**

L.G. 5. English Doeskin. Excellent washing gloves, in chamois. Elastic wrists   **10 11**

L.G. 6. Fine Fabric. With beautiful suede finish. Grey, chamois, drab, black, and white. 3-button **4 6**

L.G. 7. Pure Silk. Best quality, with double finger tips, 2-dome, black and white   **4 11**

L.G. 8. Chevrette Suede. 3-cord points, pique sewn. Beaver, grey, mole, drab, and black. 3-button **7 11**

L.G. 9. Tan Cape. Good quality, 2-button. **13 9**

L.G. 10. Chevrette Kid. Pique sewn, with black points and elastic wrists. Best quality   **14 9**

L.G. 11 Lisle Thread Children's Gloves. White, beaver, grey, and drab. 3 button   **2 3**

L.G. 12. Children's Fabric Gloves With excellent suede finish. White and drab. 2-dome   **3 3**

L.G. 13. Children's Silk Gloves. Very good quality, with double finger tips. White only. 2-dome. **3 3**

L.G. 14. Children's Antelope. Grey and tan, 1 button   **7 6**

L.G. 15. Ladies' Doeskin Gauntlets. Strap wrists, in beaver and slate   **10 11**

chamois palm country versions; their golfing gloves
had the fashionable 'cool string backs'. In the same
catalogue for 1937 they recorded that 'Informal
Chamois gloves are correct for all informal and almost
all formal occasions', and formal white capeskin
gloves need only be worn, '. . . to levees at the Palace
or Masonic dinners!'

By the end of the war, women's fashions had
assumed a more assertive, slightly more practical and
militaristic air. Skirts were shorter, hair was being

◁ 54 *Advertisement from Harrods sale catalogue,
1919. The range of colours and styles for women's
daytime gloves were limited, but the many types of
material and the variations in price domonstrate the
continuing importance of gloves in most women's
wardrobes despite the social changes brought by the
1914-18 war.*

*55 Fashions at Ascot, press photograph, June 1927.
Gloves were essential accessories for both men and
women at formal daytime events, but they were
uniformly plain; the hats and bags of the two women
are far more individualistic.*

---

bobbed, a more youthful and determined prototype
was replacing the mature, socially conservative ideal
of the pre-war years. This mood helped to reinforce
the movement towards plainer gloves which was
already evident in the pre-1914 years, but in the
1920s and 1930s the range of gloves was still very
wide. A catalogue published by Dents the glove
manufacturers in 1926 contains thirty-four pages of
text and illustrations, many of the latter in colour,
and the wide range of contents included fur, leather,
wool and fabric gloves in all conceivable colours,
both lined and unlined. Although the classic three to

GLOVES

(Illustrations 1 and 2)

(Illustration 3)

(Illustration 4)

(Illustration 5)

Tan cape kid lined with Jaeger camelhair and wool or with cashmere and pure wool, gauntlet or button, from 13 6

Fancy wool gloves in bright colours and designs, from 4 11. Also camelhair and wool gloves.

Skating gloves, from 4 6

Brushed wool, from 3 6

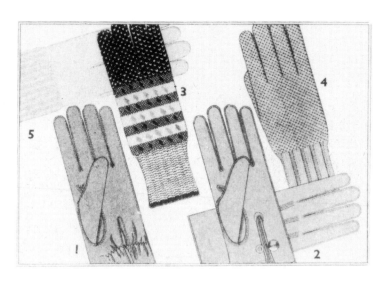

four button, close-fitting leather glove never completely disappeared, the 1920s and 1930s were, in terms of fashion gloves, the great age of the gauntlet. At first, in the 1920s there was only a hint of additional width, perhaps with a gusset inserted at the back of the glove and an elasticated wrist which helped to emphasize the new, waisted line. Decoration on these gloves was usually restricted to a small amount of contrast stitching, or the juxtaposition of different coloured leathers, either in geometrical appliqué designs or as a contrast component in the structure of the glove itself.

From the mid-1920s until the early 1930s the Art Deco movement which greatly influenced the design of fabrics, embroidery patterns and other areas of decoration, made some impact on gloves. Pretty pastel coloured suede or leather gloves were embroidered with rich glowing flowers and trellis designs in lively combinations of chenille, floss silks and beads (fig. 57). This brief renaissance of the decorated gauntlet inspired some glove manufacturers to produce exhibition gloves which copied, in a simplified

56 Advertisement from Jaeger for men. c. 1934. By this date men's gloves had reached the point of being 'classic' accessories, and these styles would not look out of place nearly fifty years later.

form, some of the complicated patterns on early seventeenth-century gauntlets. Dent Fownes have a small group of these which were produced by a French manufacturer, and although they are amusing curiosities, they seem lifeless pastiches when compared with the imaginative Art Deco designs.

Gloves were still considered an acceptable present, and advertisements often concentrated on this dimension, particularly at Christmas time. Harvey Nichols in 1934 had a two page feature in their Christmas catalogue on 'Gloves Practical and Gloves Luxurious . . . gifts that are absolutely certain of success'. The twelve styles illustrated included gloves and gauntlets of fabric, leather and fur and ranged in price from Duplex fabric gloves at 4 shillings 6 pence to fur-lined cape leather gauntlets at 35 shillings 9 pence, the 'perfect Christmas Glove'. Gauntlet gloves were the fashionable daytime choice throughout the 1930s, although knitted wool or string gloves were favoured for sporting or country wear. The majority of evening gloves were long, up to twenty button suede or kid, in a wide range of colours. Pastel shades were fashionable throughout the inter-war period, leavened by the occasional splash of vivid colour: jade green, gold, raspberry or bright blue. Some dress designers produced gloves as part of a complete outfit, either using leather with an additional feature which complemented the fabric or decoration of the dress, or they used a matching or toning fabric. Schiaparelli, the designer whose witty clothes made use of surrealistic motifs, incorporated some of these features into even the smallest accessories like gloves, and manufacturers followed her lead, in a more cautious manner by producing slashed upper arms or asymmetric colour combinations.

By December 1939, three months after the outbreak of war, Dickens and Jones's Christmas

57 Woman's gloves, 1925-30. Beige suede leather with embroidered points of red, grey and gold thread; the gauntlet embroidered with an Art Deco design of stylized flowers worked in pink and grey chenille and silver beads; French, made by Alexandrine.

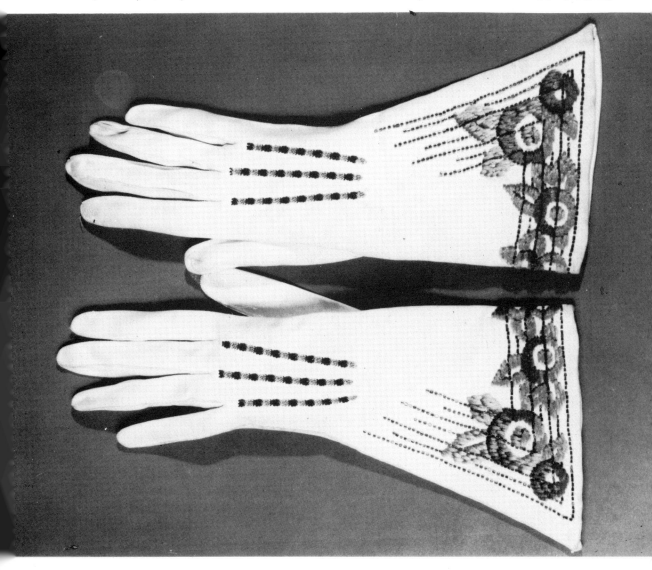

catalogue suggested that 'Gloves Make the Ideal Gift', and offered a range which cost between 6 shillings 11 pence and 21 shillings 9 pence per pair, and in the following year Harvey Nichols was still able to advertise three varieties of French glove. However, this situation could not last much longer. France fell to the Germans in 1940, and all international trade was once more disrupted by world-wide warfare. When, in Britain, clothes were rationed along with many other items in 1942, gloves were inevitably included (fig.

58). As part of an information service to the public, the Board of Trade issued, on 1 November 1943, 'The 1943-1944 Clothing Quiz' which listed the coupon requirements for particular items. A pair of gloves or mittens containing leather or fur required two coupons from a man, a woman or a child. If they did not contain leather or fur, only one coupon was needed. Amongst the list of principal coupon-free articles were 'Gloves made of asbestos; gloves made wholly or partly of rubber (except gloves in which

58 *Advertisement from a Harvey Nichols catalogue, 1941. During the 1930-45 war clothes' rationing was introduced, and all advertisements carried information about the number of coupons required for each item in addition to the price.*

59 *Advertisement from a Harvey Nichols catalogue, ▷ 1950. This photograph demonstrates how fashion can easily exaggerate or distort the appearance of other accessories, but does not ever, in any tangible way alter the basic structure of gloves.*

*W*arm Gauntlets in wool. You will want one of these for every-day wear. Brown, navy, beaver, stone, with interesting contrasting colour. (Only 1 coupon) 10/9

*H*ogskins — always so good looking with tweeds and smart all year round. Natural or oatmeal. (2 coupons). 18/9

for Ascot

A wonderful picture hat in pink crinoline, with curled ostrich feathers.
also available in navy, black or white. £9 . 9 . 0
Soft pouchy bag in grosgrain, navy or black. size 10 x 6 with 4½ in. base.
£6 . 19 . 6
Fine French suède elbow-length gloves in navy, brown, pastel pink,
grey, beige or black. £3 . 15 . 6
Elegant platform shoes in grosgrain. Navy, brown or black.
American sizes 5—8½. £5 . 9 . 6

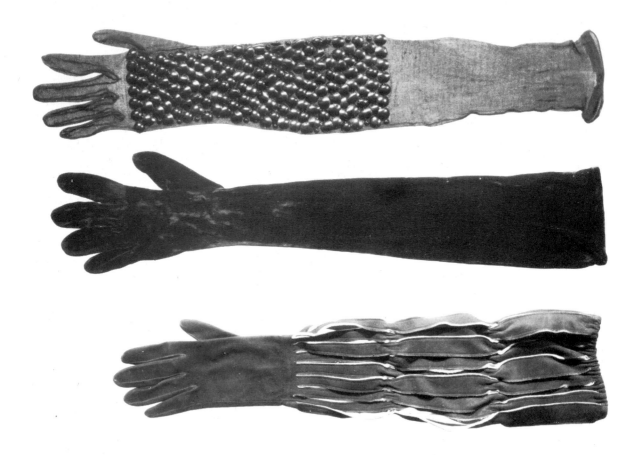

the only rubber is in the elastic in the wrist); gloves of whatever material suitable only for use as sports accessories or requisites; mittens fulfilling such conditions.'

Gloves in wartime became simple and functional, and were included amongst the range of utility items for which strict government regulations regarding content and efficient use of materials were laid down. The majority of the population managed with its pre-war gloves, or managed to acquire wool from time-to-time in order to knit gloves and mittens for home use and for troops serving overseas. Most of the glove manufacturers received orders from the government for military, naval or air-force personnel. For instance, the Ministry of Supply ordered several million pairs of special operation gloves from fabric glove manu-facturers, including pure silk Milanese gauntlets for airmen, electrically heated fabric gloves for the American Air Force, and 'mosquito-proof gloves for men fighting in the jungles of Burma.'[8]

60 Women's gloves, 1946-50. The most imaginative and witty post-war gloves were those produced in the great French couture houses; black and beige slashed gloves by Hermes; black velvet by Molyneux; black knitted silk with beads by Schiaparelli.

After the war gloves never regained the important place they had held in the wardrobes of the 1920s and 1930s. Rationing remained in Britain until the early 1950s, and all luxuries were both expensive and difficult to obtain. In addition there was a rather more realistic approach to clothing, and it began to

61 Fashion photograph, 1950-55. Elbow-length ▷ kid gloves were still the usual choice for formal evening engagements in the 1950s, although a few women were switching to cheaper, more easily washed nylon ones.

be accepted that gloves were not essential except for certain occasions and certain times of year (fig. 59). Leather gloves were much more expensive, and fabric and wool gloves, although not correct on the most formal occasions, could be worn at all other times. From the early 1950s onwards the number of advertisements for gloves in catalogues and magazines are fewer, and the type of gloves which were advertised fall into a few 'classic' categories. Wittiness, humour and imaginative design were rarely features of the industry (fig. 60).

Men's gloves from the 1950s onwards were often plain cape leather in dark colours, natural hogskin or pigskin gloves with hand-stitching, string gloves in fawn or yellow, and wool gloves, sometimes with leather palms. Crochet-back gloves with cape palms were considered 'perfect for driving', and were promoted by Harrods as 'Stirling Moss sports gloves . . . .' Lamb and sheepskin gloves became popular in the 1960s, but the ever increasing price of all gloves helped to re-kindle a spartan attitude in many men, so that by the 1970s young men hardly ever wore gloves other than for driving, and these had thin perforated leather palms with string or nylon imitation string backs and could be purchased relatively inexpensively from chain stores. Older men might still own a pair of lined cape leather or hogskin gloves or a pair of woollen gloves, but nothing more. As the price of unlined hogskin gloves had risen in price from 55 shillings in 1955 to £19.50 in 1979 this is perhaps an understandable attitude, although perhaps not understandable to a glove manufacturer, when he compares the prices that are now paid for shoes in comparison to 1955. However, in a society in which informality in dress is more admired than formality, it was inevitable that the two accessories which were most expendable, gloves and hats, would sink very low in the order of priorities as prices for all clothes rose.

Women's gloves were equally understated in appearance, and less prominent in advertising features from the mid 1950s onwards. Apart from long evening gloves (fig. 61) and bracelet-length daytime ones, the newest length of glove was closely fitting to what a Harvey Nichols catalogue referred to in 1952 as

62 *Fashion photograph, 1966. Many of the new, young designers of the 1960s rarely bothered about accessorizing their clothes, but Courrèges consistently chose short white gloves to add balance and finish to his overall look.*

'short wrist length'. Leather and suede were increasingly expensive and more mention was made of fabric gloves. In another Harvey Nichols catalogue, of 1956, a large feature on 'Accessories . . . and what to wear with them', contains a great many illustrations of hats and shoes, but only five pairs of gloves are illustrated, including wrist-length 'fabric shorties', three-quarter length suede and evening suede gloves. Within the range of fabric gloves, nylon was assuming considerable importance, and there was a vogue for 'sueded' nylon gloves.

Bracelet-length gloves retained their popularity in the early 1960s, but young women preferred short, wrist-length gloves, and with the impetus given to young fashions in that decade by the new generation of lively designers in England and France, this type of glove was the most suitable accessory (fig. 62). In the late 1960s and early 1970s, these short gloves were to be found in a wide range of bright colours using two colour combinations of leather, cut-out motifs and some appliqué work. Knitted gloves also increased in popularity as fashions became more relaxed, with variations which used different colours for each finger, or complex Fair Isle or ethnic designs.

By the late 1970s the range of gloves generally available fell into two main categories. The first category contained the classic styles, perennially popular washable leather gloves, good-quality lined cape skin, lambskin, hand-stitched hogskin and crochet cotton (or nylon) backed driving gloves. These came in the traditionally safe colours: tan, brown, stone, black and navy, with some richer colours if fashion seemed to favour particular shades (plate 7). The second category contained fabric and knitted gloves, often in a wider and livelier range of colours and patterns. The great majority of all evening gloves had changed from leather to nylon, often with a particular finish: satin, lurex, lace or net.

The major area of this century's innovation in glovemaking has very little to do with fashion. Great strides have been made in the development of protective and industrial gloves and mittens. Almost every type of heavy manual, industrial, chemical, medical or technological work has been made less dangerous for workers by the introduction of specialized coverings for the hands. Even the simple domestic versions, rubber gloves, come in more weights and finishes than ever before, and it is likely that more pairs of gloves are worn for protective purposes today, than as a fashionable accessory.

CONCLUSION

It is perhaps ironical to suggest in a conclusion to a book that this is really only the starting point for the serious connoisseur of gloves. I have attempted to indicate the major developments in the mainstream of fashionable gloves over a period of nearly four centuries, but I am conscious of leaving many avenues unexplored. There has not been space to examine the significance and evolution of ecclesiastical and ceremonial gloves, or to discuss in detail the important contribution made to the history of English glovemaking by certain parts of the country or by specific manufacturers.

The emphasis in this book has been placed on the ingenious and imaginative glovemakers of the seventeenth and nineteenth centuries. All accessories were fashionable ephemera whether cheap or expensive at the time they were made. They existed to complement or to complete a particular style of dress, and if they seemed on occasion to rise above this and assumed an identity in their own right as small exquisite objects, this is an unexpected bonus which we can appreciate today through the magnificent public collections. The finest gloves have been preserved because they impressed subsequent generations with their originality or decorative qualities which overcame the natural prejudice which is usually felt about 'old-fashioned' items.

If this book can stimulate the interest of late twentieth century glove wearers to continue the time-honoured tradition of preserving the best of modern gloves, so that they may stand alongside their ancestors in present and future sequence, it will have succeeded in its aim. Originality and ingenuity may have been replaced by functionalism, but the finest modern gloves are technically equal to the cut, stitching and finish of the best nineteenth-century ones, and should not be considered of lesser merit because of their simplicity. An understanding of the history and traditions of a craft can enrich one's appreciation of its contemporary products, and place them into the context of a changing but continuous evolution in which both the high points and the quiet practicality are of equal importance to historical perspective.

Notes

CHAPTER 1

1   B.E. Ellis, *Gloves and the Glove Trade*, p. 89;
    C. Cody Collins, *Love of a Glove*, p. 85.
    The contents of Chapter 1 include much technical
    detail, although considerably abbreviated, which
    is taken from the two books, mentioned above,
    and also from N.L. Leyland and J.E. Troughton's
    Glovemaking in West Oxfordshire, and J.W.
    Waterer's *A Guide to the Conservation and
    Restoration . . . of Leather*.
2   Leyland and Troughton, *op. cit.*, p. 11.
3   Pepys' Diary, Vol. VIII, 1667, p. 425.
4   R. Campbell, *The London Tradesman*, p. 223.
5   The Dent Fownes collection includes a certificate
    issued to a journeyman glover at the end of his
    seven year apprenticeship in 1688.
6   F.A. Wells, *The British Hosiery and Knitwear
    Industry*, pp. 78-9.
7. *Ibid.*, p. 82.
8   *Ibid.*
9   National Association of Glove Manufacturers,
    *The Story of the Fabric Glove Industry of Great
    Britain*, p. 29.
10 *Ibid.*, p. 30.
11 *Ibid.*, p. 32.
12 Ellis, *op. cit.*, p. 111.
13 Wells, *op. cit.*, p. 16.
14 *Ibid.*, p. 111.

CHAPTER 2

1   T. Hughes, *English Domestic Needlework*, p. 204.
2   J. Norton-Kyshe, *The Law and Customs Relating
    to Gloves*, p. 58.
3   Norton-Kyshe, *op. cit.*, develops these themes at
    some length, as does W.S. Beck in *Gloves, Their
    Annals and Associations*.
4   Hughes, *op. cit.*, p. 205.
5   Calendar of State Papers Venetian xv. 270 quoted
    in M.C. Linthicum, *Costume in the Drama of
    Shakespeare and his Contemporaries*, p. 270.
6   Extract from the 'Wardrobe Account of Henry,
    Prince of Wales,' *Archaeologia* 11, p. 93.

7   Quoted in Smith, *op. cit.*, p. 28.
8   Quoted in P. Cunnington and C. Lucas, *Costume
    for Births, Marriages and Deaths*, p. 67.
9   R. Strong, 'Charles I's clothes for the years 1633
    to 1635', *Costume* 14, pp. 85, 88.
10 Smith, *op. cit.*, p. 31.
11 P. and A. Mactaggart, 'The Rich Wearing Apparel
    of Richard, 3rd Earl of Dorset, *Costume* 14,
    p. 49.
12 Strong, *op. cit.*, p. 82.
13 *Ibid.*, p. 88.
14 Pepys' Diary, Vol. VIII, 1667, p. 322.
15 *Ibid.*, p. 425.
16 *Ibid.*, p. 134.
17 F.P. and M.M. Verney, eds, *Memoirs of the
    Verney Family*, Vol. 4, p. 327.
18 Cunnington & Lucas, *op. cit.*, p. 193.
19 N. Penney, ed., *Household Account Book of
    Sarah Fell of Swarthmoor Hall*, p. 69.
20 Quoted in Hughes, *op. cit.*, p. 207.
21 Quoted in N. Waugh, *The Cut of Men's Clothes*,
    p. 49.

CHAPTER 3

1   Quoted in C.W. & P. Cunnington, *Handbook of
    English Costume in the 18th Century*, p. 176.
2   *Ibid.*
3   *Ibid.*
4   Quoted in Cunnington, *op. cit.*, p. 261.
5   *Ibid.*, p. 97.
6   Quoted in Cunnington & Lucas, *op. cit.*, p. 193.
7   *Ibid.*, p. 196.
8   Quoted in Hughes, *op. cit.*, p. 207.
9   Quoted in Cunnington, *op. cit.*, p. 397.
10 From a trade card in the Museum of London.
11 Wells, *op. cit.*, p. 75.
12 Quoted in Cunnington, *op. cit.*, p. 397.
13 *Ibid.*
14 Mrs V.D. Broughton, ed., *The Journals of Mrs
    Papendiek*, Vol. I, pp. 313-14.
15 From a trade card in the Museum of London.

16 *Ibid.*
17 *Ibid.*
18 Quoted in Cunnington, *op. cit.*, p. 177.
19 P. Clabburn, 'A Provincial Milliner's Shop in 1785', *Costume* **11**, pp. 100-112.
20 Smith, *op. cit.*, p. 63.
21 *Ibid.*
22 Wells, *op. cit.*, p. 229.
23 Ellis, *op. cit.*, p. 124.
24 Smith, *op. cit.*, p. 64.

CHAPTER 4
1 Anon., *Etiquette for Ladies*, p. 8.
2 Anon., *Hints on Etiquette*, p. 51.
3 *Ibid.*, p. 41.
4 *Ibid.*, p. 31.
5 *Etiquette for Ladies*, p. 8.
6 *Ibid.*, p. 34.
7 Quoted in C.W. Cunnington, *English Women's Clothing in the 19th Century*, p. 22.
8 *Ibid.*, p. 282.
9 *Hints on Etiquette*, p. 31.
10 Advertisement placed by the Nottingham Warehouse in *La Belle Assemblée*, 1806.
11 Quoted in Cunnington, *op. cit.*, p. 42.
12 *Ibid.*, p. 46.
13 Smith, *op. cit.*, p. 58.
14 Ellis, *op. cit.*, pp. 20-21.
15 Smith, *op. cit.*, p. 77.
16 Quoted in Cunnington, *op. cit.*, p. 113.
17 I am indebted to Miss Sarah Levitt who has kindly allowed me to include some of her research findings from these patent registers in this chapter.

18 PRO, BT45-1/146; PRO, BT-1/176.
19 PRO, BT43.386, class 12 ii, 33847.
20 Quoted in C.W. & P. Cunnington, *Handbook of English Costume in the 19th Century*, p. 226.
21 *Ibid.*, p. 282.
22 Anon., *Glove Story*, p. 8.
23 PRO, BT43-422/75601; PRO, BT43-422/75741.
24 PRO, BT43.427/206230.
25 PRO, BT43.427/209561.
26 Quoted in C.W. Cunnington, *op. cit.*, p. 263.
27 PRO, BT43-430, 308/41-43.
28 Quoted in C.W. Cunnington, *op. cit.*, p. 324.
29 Mrs J. Sherwood, *Manners and Social Usages*, quoted in C.W. & P. Cunnington, *Costume for Births, Marriages and Deaths*, p. 116.
30 Quoted in C.W. Cunnington, *op. cit.*, p. 324
31 *Ladies' Gazette of Fashion*, July 1879, p. 186.
32 D. Alexander, *Retailing in England during the Industrial Revolution*, p. 241.
33 A. Adburgham, *Shops and Shopping 1800-1914*, p. 109.
34 C.W. Cunnington, *op. cit.*, p. 411.

CHAPTER 5
1 Ellis, *op. cit.*, p. 21.
2 Smith, *op. cit.*, p. 93.
3 Ellis, *op. cit.*, p. 114.
4 The Diaries of Lady Cynthia Asquith, p. 189.
5 A. Mansfield & P. Cunnington, *Handbook of English Costume in the 20th Century*, p. 96.
6 Ellis, *op. cit.*, p. 29.
7 *Ibid.*, p. 30.
8 National Association of Glove Manufacturers, *op. cit.*, pp. 33, 71.

Glossary

Antelope   a fine-quality leather with a velvety suede nap, finished on the flesh side of antelope or gazelle skins.

Berlins   German imported leather gloves, similar to Woodstock gloves. 'White Berlins' were strong white cotton gloves, easily washed and particularly suitable for household servants.

Cape   initially a soft gloving leather made from South African hair sheepskins from the Cape and Port Elizabeth districts. The term was later applied to similar hair sheepskin leathers from elsewhere.

Chickenskin   lightweight leather made from the skin of unborn calves; c.f. Limericks.

Cordinent/cordwain   a soft leather made originally in Spain from hair sheepskins or goatskins. The term was used in England to describe home-produced leathers which resembled the Spanish originals.

Doeskin   leather made from lightweight deerskins, not necessarily just does, and oil tanned.

Doling   the term for thinning certain areas of a skin with a sharp knife to produce a lighter, more supple leather.

Dogskin   heavyweight sheepskin leather used for hunting or hawking gloves.

Fourchette   the narrow strip of leather in a glove which forms the inside of the finger.

'In the white'   tanned or tawed skins before they are dyed and finished.

Jessamy   a jasmine scent for gloves, often in the form of jessamy butter which could be smoothed onto the inside of the glove.

Limericks   chickenskin gloves from Limerick in Ireland.

Mocha   an expensive velvety leather, finished on the grain side of Arabian hair sheepskin.

Nappa   a full grain leather made of sheep, lamb or kidskins treated with a mineral tannage.

Paring   the term for reducing the thickness of the backs of skins using a saucer-shaped knife.

Pointing   the lines of decoration on the back of the glove, most correctly the three horizontal rows of stitching.

Quirks   small leather gussets sometimes fitted at the base of the fingers and thumb to allow more flexibility of movement.

Shammy   a soft leather initially made from chamois antelopes, but later simulated with sheep and lambskins using an oil tannage and capable of being washed.

Spangles   small sequin-like decorations made of metal and used on embroideries.

Staking   the term for rendering leather more supply by passing it over a blunt, rounded blade supported on a beam or post.

Suede   leather finished with a nap on the flesh side, a coarser finish than leather with a nap on the grain side.

Tabs   the separated panels on the gauntlets of seventeenth-century gloves.

Tanning/tawing   the process of dressing skins to preserve them using barks and berries (vegetable tannage); oil or mineral (alum, chrome, formaldehyde).

Trank   the piece of leather from which the gloves are cut.

Wash leather   another term for shammy or chamois leather.

Woodstocks   gloves made in Woodstock from the skins of fawns or does and washable.

York tans   gloves of natural coloured suede.

Select Bibliography

Adburgham, A.   *Shops and Shopping 1800-1914,*
   George Allen & Unwin, 1964

Alexander, D.   *Retailing in England During the*
   Industrial Revolution,   Athlone Press, 1970

Anon.   *Glove Story,*   Dents, n.d.

Anon.   *A Short History of . . . The Glovers*
   Company,   London, 1950

Anon.   *The Story of the Fabric Glove Industry of*
   Great Britain,   National Association of Glove
   Manufacturers, 1949

Beck, S.W.   *Gloves, Their Annals and Associations,*
   London, 1883

Buck, A.   *Victorian Costume and Costume*
   Accessories,   Herbert Jenkins, 1961

Clark, F.   *Challenge to Fashion, Gloves 1600-1979,*
   Worthing Museum, 1979

Cody Collins, C.   *Love of a Glove,*   New York,
   1947

Cunnington, C.W.   *English Women's Clothing in the*
   19th Century,   Faber and Faber, 1937

Cunnington, C.W. & P.   *Handbook of English*
   Costume in the 18th Century,   Faber & Faber,
   1966

Cunnington, C.W. & P.   *Handbook of English*
   Costume in the 19th Century,   Faber & Faber,
   1973

Cunnington, P. & Lucas, C.   *Costume for Births,*
   Marriages & Deaths,   A & C Black, 1972

Ellis, B.E. *Gloves and the Glove Trade,*   Pitman &
   Sons, 1921

English, W.   *The Textile Industry,* Longmans, 1969

Foster, V.   'A Garden of Flowers', *Costume* **14**,
   Costume Society, 1980

Hughes, T.   *English Domestic Needlework,*   Abbey
   Fine Arts, 1961

Hull, W.   *History of the Glove Trade,* London, 1834

Lawrence, G.H.M.   *Herbals, Their History and*
   Significance,   The Clark Memorial Library & The
   Hunt Botanical Library, 1965

Leyland, N.L. & Troughton, J.E.   *Glovemaking in*
   West Oxfordshire,   Oxford City and County
   Museum, 1974

Mansfield, A. & Cunnington, P.   *Handbook of*
   English Costume in the 20th Century 1900-1950,
   A & C Black, 1973

Mason, S.G. ed.   *British Hosiery and Knitwear,*
   National Trade Press, 1947

Norton-Kyshe, J.W.   *The Law and Customs Relating*
   to Gloves,   London, 1901

Smith, W.M.   *Gloves Past and Present,*   New York,
   1918

Spiers, C.H.   'Deer Skin Leathers and Their Use for
   Costume', *Costume* **VII**,   Costume Society, 1973

Waterer, J.W.   *A Guide to the Conservation &*
   Restoration . . . of Leather,   G Bell & Sons, 1972

Wells, F.A.   *The British Hosiery and Knitwear*
   Industry, David & Charles, 1972

Index